Gladstone

B H Abbott

Collins London and Glasgow

General Editors
K H Randell   J W Hunt
© B H Abbott 1972

Printed in Great Britain
Collins Clear Type Press
Set in Monotype Plantin

ISBN 0 00 327210 9

First published 1972
Fourth impression 1978

Cover illustration: Radio Times Hulton Picture Library

Contents

Editors' foreword

The series of which this book is a part is designed to meet the needs of students in Sixth Forms and those taking courses in further and higher education. In assessing these needs two factors especially have been taken into account: the limits on the student's time which preclude the reading of all the important scholarly works, and the importance of providing stimulus to thought and imagination. Therefore the series, which has considerably more space available than even the larger single-volume textbooks on the period, presents the interpretations which have altered or increased our understanding of the age, as well as including sufficient detail to illustrate and enliven the subject. Most important of all, emphasis has been placed on discussion. Instead of outlining supposedly established facts, problems are posed as they were faced by the people of the time and as they confront the historian today in his task of interpretation. The student is thus enabled to approach the subject in an attitude of enquiry, and is encouraged to exercise his own mind on the arguments, never closed, of historiography. In so doing he will gain some knowledge of the methods of historians and of the kinds of evidence they use. He should also find enjoyment by the way.

The arrangement of the series, with several volumes covering particular aspects over a long period, and others with more strict chronological limits, has enabled each author to concentrate on an area of special interest, and should make for flexibility in use by the reader.

K.H.R.
J.W.H.

Full details of historical works referred to in the text will be found in the list of books suggested for further reading on page 157. Only where the work is not included is a full reference given in the text.

Chapter 1

Beginnings and ends—a survey

Benjamin Disraeli (1804-81) and William Ewart Gladstone (1809-98) dominated English politics in the seventh and eighth decades of the nineteenth century. Gladstone, the 'Grand Old Man', as his colleague and successor Lord Rosebery called him, was to remain a leading figure until his final retirement in 1894. In an age without film, television or 'pop' stars, and without football champions, the nation found its heroes and villains in the House of Commons, and the extension of the right to vote in 1867 intensified the popular interest in politics. Disraeli and Gladstone were pre-eminent in the publicity and clamour that accompanied politics in the first dawn of the age of the common man. Their mutual antipathy, their verbal duels and their opposing policies led to the first comparisons and contrasts being drawn between them. In recent years, however, historians have paid more attention to an analysis of their individual policies, and to the assessment of their unique contribution to political events than to comparisons which, nonetheless, seem inevitable. In the elections of 1868, 1874 and 1880 the voters, in choosing between the two parties that they led, were perhaps the first to estimate the comparative worth of Gladstone and Disraeli as leaders of the nation, and it is still difficult to escape from the fascination of the problem. Where does the conflict begin?

It is not only Disraeli's attachment to Conservatism and Gladstone's to Liberalism that provide a contrast. They were men from two different aspects of the same world. Gladstone was a reflection of the idealistic and earnest aspects of Victorian society, the belief in progress, whilst Disraeli reflected the romantic and escapist aspects, the belief in tradition. Gladstone was a member of a wealthy merchant family based in Liverpool, with interests in India, America and the West Indies, as well as large estates in Flintshire. He was educated at Eton and Christ Church, Oxford. Disraeli's background was Jewish and literary. His father, who had been received into the Church of England, had written a book, *The Curiosities of Literature*, and Disraeli himself had published the first parts of his first novel, *Vivian Grey*, in 1826. Disraeli's was not the best of springboards into politics. Apart from his ethnic origins, he had been educated privately and did not go to a university.

Gladstone first attracted political attention to himself when, as President of the Oxford Union in 1831, he successfully opposed in debate a motion on the need for parliamentary reform—though in later years he blamed his success in that debate for delaying his acceptance of Liberalism. In that year Disraeli published his third novel, *The Young Duke*. Both managed the Grand Tour before the 1832 election. Significantly Disraeli visited Egypt and the East, the scene of one of his later triumphs, and Gladstone made his first visit to Italy, a country which was to have a profound effect upon his political outlook. The election of 1832 saw Gladstone successfully returned as one of the Members of Parliament for the Duke of Newcastle's rotten borough of Newark. Disraeli fought two unsuccessful elections as a Radical at High Wycombe and in the County of Buckinghamshire. In 1833, whilst Gladstone was taking up residence in the Albany and joining the Conservative Carlton Club, Disraeli fought a third unsuccessful election. Gladstone's political career had begun almost automatically, whilst Disraeli had to console himself with lounging and pleasure, until he was returned to Parliament at the fourth attempt in 1837 as the second Conservative candidate for Maidstone.

Gladstone had taken the slavery issue as his platform in the 1832 election, and though he supported the idea of emancipation, he hoped it would be gradual. His own family's West Indian plantations had made him well aware that many Negro slaves were better treated than many of the industrial workers in English factories. A newspaper, publishing an imaginary conversation with Disraeli when he stood for election unsuccessfully at Marylebone, remarked: 'Someone asked Disraeli in offering himself for Marylebone on what he intended to stand. "On my head", was the reply'. Although a quip rather than a fact the comment does reflect Disraeli's seeming lack of political purpose as he wandered around seeking a seat and a party. It may have been these unfortunate early experiences as a prospective candidate that led Disraeli to regard politics in his more cynical moods as a dirty game—they certainly provided his enemies with material for their characterisation of him as a scheming politician. Gladstone's comparatively meteoric rise in politics, however, may well have done him a disservice in preventing him from discovering the mundane realities of political life. Gladstone's moral principles on more than one occasion were to prevent him from facing the realities of human nature, and his early success encouraged his priggishness. He was able to take a high moral tone, but in the end his lack of experience of the in-fighting of party politics was to prove a handicap.

The two men first met in 1835 at a dinner party given by Lord Lyndhurst. Disraeli was still not a Member of Parliament, whilst Gladstone was already a Junior Lord of the Treasury, if only briefly, in Peel's first government. Disraeli noted in a letter to his sister the presence of Gladstone as 'a swan', who was the best company there. Gladstone, however, took no special notice of Disraeli, though later he recalled that Disraeli had been dressed foppishly and was very dull.

Gladstone was disappointed when he was not offered Cabinet rank in Peel's ministry of 1841, but he was not as disappointed as Disraeli, whose request for a junior post was refused. Robert Blake in his biography of Disraeli has pointed out that 'by the standards of his day Peel was acting perfectly reasonably in ignoring Disraeli, just as Disraeli, by the same standards, was acting unreasonably in expecting anything else'. The rebuff certainly coloured Disraeli's critical attitude to Peel, even if it did not create it. By 1845 Disraeli, perhaps worried by his lack of prospects and seeing Peel's control of the Conservative party as an obstacle to his own advancement, had begun a series of attacks on Peel that were to culminate in the Corn Law debates. These attacks created the first breach in the political relations between Gladstone and Disraeli, an incurable breach as far as Gladstone was concerned.

During the same period Gladstone was moving closer to Peel. The connections of Gladstone's father with the Tory party assured the son a place in that party, just as the father's friendship with Peel brought the son quickly to the attention of the leader of the party. It was in his capacities as Vice-President and later as President of the Board of Trade that Gladstone provided the facts and figures for Peel's fiscal reforms, and at the same time found himself converted to free trade. Yet in 1845 Gladstone resigned over the Maynooth Question. In his book *Church and State* he had criticised the original grant made by the Whigs to pay for Maynooth College, a seminary for the training of Roman Catholic clergy. He had since changed his mind, but Peel's intention to increase the grant embarrassed him. Disraeli, amongst others, believed that Gladstone's resignation had ruined his career, but at the end of 1845 Peel invited Gladstone to join as Colonial Secretary the new Cabinet he had formed after the split over the Corn Laws. For many historians with the benefit of hindsight there was already ample proof that Disraeli was a cynical dilletante and Gladstone a man of honour.

Disraeli's attack on Peel was based not on opposition to the repeal of the Corn Laws, on which Disraeli had no firm convictions and on which he could not be sure of winning enough support, but rather on the notion that Peel had betrayed the Conservative party. Disraeli made his views very clear: 'Let men stand by the principle by which they rise, right or wrong. I make no exception. If they be wrong, they must retire to that shade of private life with which our present rulers have so often threatened us. . . Above all maintain the line of demarcation between parties, for it is only by maintaining the independence of party that you can maintain the integrity of public men, and the power and influence of Parliament itself.' This was not only damning criticism but also a prophetic view of the way political parties were to emerge in the future, especially after 1868, when Disraeli and Gladstone were to face each other across the floor of the House of Commons as bitter rivals. Indeed A. J. P. Taylor has given Disraeli credit for first making clear the importance of the strict line of demarcation between the political parties, between the government and the opposition.

Peel managed to repeal the Corn Laws, but lost the vote on a Coercion Bill for Ireland and resigned. The Conservative party, newly created by Peel, was split into Protectionists led by Derby, and Peelites roughly grouped under Lord Aberdeen. Gladstone's support for Peel seemed to have excluded him from political power, whilst Disraeli had propelled himself into the hierarchy of the Conservative party, even if the rest of the hierarchy regarded him with suspicion or bemused tolerance. Even then his pre-eminence in the House of Commons was not assured until the death in 1848 of his friend Lord George Bentinck, who had led the attack on Peel. Both men had distinguished themselves in the assault on their leader's political position, but most respectable Conservatives preferred the lordly Bentinck to the foppish Disraeli.

Much attention has been focused on Disraeli's treatment of Peel. To his adherents Disraeli was defending Conservatism and principle; to his critics he destroyed Peel merely for his own political advantage. Unfortunately the conclusion reached on this problem has tended to colour all other verdicts on Disraeli's career, instead of each aspect of that career being judged on its own merits. Sir Robert Peel had saved the old Tory party from a dismal death after the 1832 Reform Act by accepting the principle of reform, which he saw as the adaptation of traditional institutions to meet the new conditions. It has been argued by Disraeli's critics that the destruction of Peel's government left the Conservatives in the political wilderness for nearly thirty years. Those who admire Disraeli claim that he contributed as much if not more to the evolution of Conservatism as Peel, that it was Disraeli who used the thirty years before 1874 to push the

Conservative party towards innovation and to school it in new methods of dealing with new problems, as is revealed in his policies on empire and parliamentary and social reform. The radicalism of contemporary Conservatism certainly seems to owe much to Disraeli. The idea of 'Tory democracy' may have been a romantic notion in the 1860s, but it is a commonplace in the 1970s. It was ironical that Disraeli's radical approach carried with him the Ultra-Tories, those reactionary members of the party anxious to preserve the eighteenth-century basis of the constitution and society. Thus the different social backgrounds of the two men, and their opposite attitudes to Peel, propelled them towards different political ends and ideals. What were the essential differences between the Conservatism of Disraeli and Gladstonian Liberalism?

Disraeli regarded Liberalism as an alien scourge; he branded it as cosmopolitan and continental, opposed to the national interest: 'Liberal opinions are the opinions of those who would be free from constraint and regulations, from a certain dependence and duty which are deemed necessary for the general or popular welfare. Liberal opinions are very convenient opinions for the rich or powerful.' In contrast he saw Conservatism leading Britain forward to its natural destiny without the aid of any suspect borrowing of ideas from Europe: 'I have always considered that the Tory party was the national party of England. It is not formed on a combination of oligarchs and philosophers who practise on the sectarian prejudices of a portion of the people. It is formed of all classes from the highest to the most homely, and it upholds a series of institutions that are in theory, and ought to be in practice, an embodiment of the national requirements and the security of national rights.' Increasingly Disraeli saw his task as making the natural leaders of society accept their task of leadership, and bring the people to their reward not by providing opportunities for self-improvement, but by direct government intervention. There was much in Disraeli's philosophy that was deliberately vote-catching. After all his aim in politics was to secure a working majority for the party after its disruption in 1846. But it became clear that the Conservative cause under the management of Disraeli was to preserve those valid institutions of the nation, the Crown, the Church, the Aristocracy, which the landed gentry could no longer preserve, by bringing the mass of the nation within the pale of government legislation.

Gladstone concluded after Disraeli's death that Tory democracy, the new Conservatism, was 'a demagogism not ennobled by love and the appreciation of liberty, but applied in the worst way to put down pacific, law-respecting, economic elements which ennobled the old Conservatism (of Peel), living upon the fomentation of angry passions, and still in secret as obstinately attached as ever to the evil principle of class interests'. In contrast, Liberalism for Gladstone was not merely a political philosophy but also an expression in practical human terms of the will of God. Gladstone was essentially a landowner with large estates in Flintshire. Liberalism became for him the creed of the country gentleman made militant and energetic. He personified the moral and social responsibilities of the squire transferred to politics. He was Squire Alworthy as Prime Minister. Liberalism was essentially a belief in progress combined with a belief that individuals were all equal in the sight of God. Philip Magnus in his biography of Gladstone has pointed out that 'Gladstone's true interests were outside politics, and as he grew older politics disgusted him more and more'. It is difficult to separate Gladstone from his God. Politics appear to have been a means to an end, the end being to instil into the mass of the community a consciousness of their own moral responsibility. Through Liberalism God's divine plan for society was being revealed. Historical development for Gladstone was 'the evolution of purpose steadfastly maintained and advancing towards some consummation . . . the Christian scheme'. He believed that he and the Liberal party had a duty to assist towards that consummation.

Their different political ideals are most clearly revealed in the attitudes of the two men to domestic reform. Basically Gladstone sought to provide opportunities for all to play their part in the inevitable progress of society envisaged by Liberalism. His method was to attempt to provide the right moral and material conditions which would enable the state to open the doors to self-improvement; the individual must then choose for himself. In his study of the formation of the Liberal party John Vincent has pointed out that: 'The great moral ideal of liberalism was manliness, the rejection of the various forms of patronage, from soup and blankets upwards, which had formerly been the normal part of the greatest number.' Hence Gladstone's concern for Ireland, labouring under great difficulties of intolerance and inequality, and his support for the principle of equality of opportunity in all Liberal legislation from education to the abolition of the purchase of commissions in the army. Hence also his lack of interest in the practical reforms of his colleagues, especially the radical programmes of Joseph Chamberlain. To Gladstone social reform, or 'construction' as he called it, was 'taking into the hands of the State the business of the individual man'. The State could point the way to social improvement, but it ought not to push the individual in that direction.

The Conservative party was compelled by the widening of the franchise to develop and organise new sources of electoral power. The traditional Conservative strength in the counties was not sufficient to give the party a majority, whilst the old alliance of landlord and tenant, which was the basis of this strength, was beginning to crack in the 1870s under the impact of agricultural depression. Except in Lancashire the Conservatives had not done well in the 1868 election amongst the newly enfranchised masses. From 1872 Disraeli chose to appeal to the new class of voters in the larger boroughs with a policy of social reform, and in particular of public health. It was Disraeli who pointed out that: 'In a progressive country change is constant; and the great question is, not whether you should resist change which is inevitable, but whether that change should be carried out in deference to the manners, the customs, the laws, the traditions of the people, or in deference to abstract principles and arbitrary and general doctrines.' He believed that the working classes preferred the practical social reforms the Conservatives offered to the doctrinaire and intangible reforms of the Liberals. This is still the view of the Conservatives, faced with the ideology of the Labour party.

Once Disraeli became Prime Minister again in 1874 the bulk of his domestic legislation was directed towards the urban workers. For Disraeli this had a double virtue. It made him popular in the country and it made him popular in the party. The defeat of the Liberals in 1874 had made clear the danger of offending vested interests, and the Conservative party had more than its fair share of vested interests. Disraeli could not commit political suicide by attacking privilege, and dismissed most of Gladstone's achievements in this direction as mere 'plundering and blundering'. Social reform not only won new voters but also did not offend the traditional supporters of the party, who had generally county rather than urban connections. Disraeli wanted to have his cake and eat it.

If the function of Gladstone's Liberal party could be summarised in the one word 'progress', then in an age of increasing class warfare Disraeli's bid for popular support for the Conservative party was an attempt to make his party's function one of reconciliation. 'The Tory party', he said in 1863, 'is only in its proper position when it represents popular principles. Then it is truly irresistible. Then it can uphold the throne and the altar, and majesty of the Empire, the liberty of the nation, and the rights of the multitude. There is nothing mean, paltry or exclusive, about the real character of Toryism. It necessarily depends upon enlarged sympathies and noble aspirations, because it is essentially national.' Once again this function of reconciliation is still very much at the heart of contemporary Conservatism. Disraeli stressed national principles as opposed to the 'foreign' extravagances of Liberalism, just as some members of the present party stress these same principles against the alleged extravagances of a Socialism said to be no less 'foreign'.

Practical social reforms carried out in a spirit of reconciliation made sure of the Conservative party's survival and its association with democracy. Disraeli was the catalyst through which the metamorphosis took place. However, Disraeli did not invent the term 'Tory democracy', which was first used in the 1880s by Lord Randolph Churchill, nor did he invent the attitude of mind expressed in it. Individual Tory humanitarians such as Shaftesbury, Oastler and Sadler had led the way in the first half of the nineteenth century. Carlyle and Coleridge had attempted to give the movement a literary basis, but it was Disraeli who made it an essential plank in the Conservative platform. Unencumbered by ideology the Conservative party has survived whilst its more doctrinaire rivals, whether Whig, Liberal or Socialist, must struggle to reconcile principles with political reality.

Buckle and other admiring biographers such as André Maurois saw in Disraeli's policies a new platform from which the people were to be won over to the Crown, Aristocracy, Church and Empire, but they, like Disraeli himself, exaggerated its uniqueness in order to provide a contrast with Liberal policies. It is true the Liberals tended to offer the excitement of partisanship in a demonstrably superior moral cause rather than radical improvements in living conditions, but this moral cause included justice in social arrangements, and Liberal spokesmen, including Gladstone and Bright as well as Chamberlain, always implied that their political justification lay in improving the welfare of the people. It is true that the Liberals under Gladstone came nowhere near to creating a welfare state, but nor did the Conservatives under Disraeli. To apply the accepted social welfare standards of the 1970s to the 1870s is to be unfair to both Gladstone and Disraeli, for the missionary approach of the Liberals no more resembles twentieth-century attitudes than does the romanticism of Disraeli's social policy.

Gladstone and the Liberals believed that the condition of the people could best be improved by peace, retrenchment and free trade. Even so the Liberal governments did not simply adopt a policy of laissez-faire towards practical reform, as the exaggerations of those who support the myth of Tory democracy would argue. This can be seen in the Liberals' supervision of workhouses, in their public health and trade union legislation, in the proposals of Joseph Chamberlain, and also in their concern for working-class literacy and the attempt to control the drink trade. The Conservatives carried some excellent Acts in the years 1874-6, but it was unjust and dishonest of Disraeli's admirers to let him alone wear the mantle of social reform.

The extent of Conservative and Liberal commitment to social reform, and the motives behind it, remain a matter of debate. There would seem to be less uncertainty, however, about the party responsible for parliamentary reform, and the Liberals with their Whig adherents are often given the credit. Even though a Conservative government was in power when the 1867 Reform Act was passed, the introduction of urban democracy is usually attributed to Gladstone's tactics in opposition. H. J. Hanham, however, in his essay on parliamentary reform in the nineteenth century, notes that in 1832, 1867 and 1884 the parliamentary reform acts were passed only when there was so much agreement between the parties that change was inevitable. Politicians, whether Liberal or Conservative, seemed to care only that their own supporters be enfranchised, and that the distribution of seats should reflect the distribution of power in the country. The Liberal legend that they alone were responsible for the enfranchisement of the people is no more an accurate view of their achievements than the Conservative claim to be the sole exponents of social reform.

There is less doubt, however, about Disraeli's success and Gladstone's failure in their relationships with Queen Victoria. Although the Queen recognised that they were both men of extraordinary ability, she favoured Disraeli and strongly disapproved of Gladstone. Once again the contrast between the two men is not only one of temperament but lies in the different approaches they took to the problems of the monarchy. Whilst Disraeli was eventually allowed to write to the Queen in the first person and to be seated during his audiences, Gladstone always had to follow strictly the proper court etiquette, and the Queen often found it necessary to have a précis made of his ponderous, complex and formal communications.

From the first moment of taking office Disraeli formed a relationship with the Queen to which there is no parallel in her long reign. Her great regard for Lord Melbourne whilst she was still a young queen was based on respect for his age and maturity, but her sympathy for Disraeli seems to have been based on the frivolous pleasure she found in his flattery. Unlike Gladstone,

Disraeli appreciated that the Queen was a woman and could be flattered, even to the extent of suggesting that she should become Patroness of the Artisans' Dwellings Company. During Gladstone's first ministry the Queen was not hostile to him personally; it was his policies she disliked, both domestic and foreign. Such policies were for the Queen inimical to the prestige of the monarchy, and Gladstone's ability to arouse militant democracy, as revealed by the Bulgarian crisis of 1876, perturbed her, especially as she was violently pro-Turk.

The Royal Titles Act of 1876, which made the Queen Empress of India, was basically a counterblast to the threat of Russian invasion. It may be doubted whether it made any difference to the average Indian. However, it pleased and flattered the Queen. Many Liberals, led by Robert Lowe, took exception to the measure, and this helped to fix the anti-Liberal bias of the Queen's later years. Gladstone's attack on the Turks intensified the Queen's pathological distrust of him, and by 1877 she had concluded that only insanity could explain his behaviour. In 1880 she tried desperately to avoid sending for Gladstone as successor to Disraeli, writing to her secretary that she 'would sooner abdicate than send for or have anything to do with that half-mad firebrand who would soon ruin everything and be a Dictator'. Gladstone's later lack of decision over the Sudan and his support of Home Rule for Ireland served to reinforce the Queen's assessment of him. Clearly Disraeli had no need to create a personal prejudice against Gladstone by deliberately disparaging him to the Queen, and there is no evidence that he ever tried to do so. 'However', as Magnus has remarked, 'Gladstone's position was weakened by Disraeli's unscrupulous encouragement of the Queen's partisan tendencies, which were very feminine but quite unconstitutional.'

Magnus has also pointed out that Gladstone attempted to acclimatise the monarchy to an increasingly democratic age by trying to persuade the Queen to abandon her mourning, and also to allow the Prince of Wales to play a greater part in public life. He failed, and though Disraeli's flattery succeeded to some extent where Gladstone did not, such flattery fortified the Queen's self-confidence and condoned the reversion to an unsympathetic

Hanoverian type of monarchy. All subsequent British sovereigns and Prime Ministers have accepted Gladstone's view. It has perhaps transformed the monarchy constitutionally into a rubber stamp, but it has at least heightened its moral and emotional appeal.

On Church matters also both men adopted a policy of moderation. Despite his deep religious convictions Gladstone was able to see the need for common-sense reforms in such matters as the Irish Church, the Universities Test Act, and education. Disraeli was of necessity a defender of the established Church, but he was not prepared to allow the Church to dictate to him on matters of policy, and the one attempt to reverse Liberal legislation on education, an Endowed Schools Act Amendment Bill, was dropped on Disraeli's intervention. Tolerance was becoming a virtue of statesmen.

The conduct of British foreign policy by Gladstone and Disraeli again raises an element of controversey. Disraeli is often depicted as the upholder of the traditional principles of British foreign policy—suspicious of France, alarmed by Russia, anxious to preserve Turkey, preferring to keep out of European entanglements as long as British interests were not involved. His concern with Egypt and the East had little to do with his Jewish ancestry, as some commentators, including Lord Cromer, have implied, but rather with his contribution to the Eastern Question, which loomed large also in the deliberations of the Younger Pitt, Canning and Palmerston. In contrast Gladstone is often associated with a policy which sought to deflect the course of British foreign policy from the narrow path of Palmerston. Gladstone believed in the equal rights of all nations, views which he made clear in his Midlothian electoral campaign of 1879: 'But in point of right all are equal, and you have no right to set up a system under which one is to be placed under moral suspicion or espionage, or made the subject of constant invective. If you do that, and especially if you claim for yourself a pharisaical superiority . . . you may talk about your patriotism as you please, but you are a misjudging friend of your country and are undermining the basis of esteem and respect of others for it.' Gladstone, like Hobbes, saw the relationships between powers as a natural state of anarchy, and he sought to bring the light of Christian principles to the darkness of foreign affairs. These principles he called the rule of law. It seemed a refreshing if not always a wise approach, for, as Magnus has pointed out, 'Gladstone never understood that high moral principles, in their application to foreign policy, are often more destructive of political stability than motives of national self-interest.'

The part played, however, by Gladstone's 'high moral principles' has tended to be exaggerated. The greater part of his moral outbursts on foreign affairs were made when he was in opposition, and, in opposing Palmerston, Gladstone found a colleague with similar views in Disraeli! Indeed it is a common tactic of all oppositions in attacking a government's foreign policy to adopt a 'holier than thou' attitude. As Prime Minister Gladstone could no more afford to neglect essential British interests in supporting the rights of other nations than any other Prime Minister. This is made clear in his handling of Egypt and the Sudan in his second ministry. Historians in the 1920s and 1930s, including R. W. Seton-Watson, praised Gladstone for his internationalism, seeing him as a link between the diplomacy by conference established by Castlereagh and the ideals of the League of Nations. Similarly, patriotic admirers of Disraeli stressed his independent defence of British interests. Such views still tend to distort the images of the two men.

It would be wrong, however, to deny entirely the influence upon Gladstone of his strict moral code and its effect upon his approach to all the political problems that faced him. Similarly Disraeli's romanticism, his vision of Britain as the guardian of justice, peace and honour, affected his approach to politics, and nowhere is this more apparent than in his imperial policies. To the mystical Tory concepts of Throne, Church, Aristocracy and People, Disraeli added Empire. By the end of the nineteenth century Britain had ennobled a mere commercial empire by adding the glory of simple territorial possession. Disraeli invented neither the Empire nor imperialism, but he was one of the men who added the concept of duty, later immortalised by Kipling as 'the white man's burden'. Disraeli pointed out in a speech to the House of Lords that all the communities of the Empire 'agree in recognising the commanding spirit of these islands that has formed and fashioned in such a manner so great a proportion of the globe . . . but it is not a heritage that can only be enjoyed; it must be maintained, and it can only be maintained by the same qualities that created it—by courage, by discipline, by patience, and by a reverence for public law and a respect for national rights'. Like the feudal bond, possession of colonial territory involved obligations as well as privileges for the colonial overlord. The problem for the electorate was straightforward: 'It is whether you will be content to be a comfortable England, modelled and moulded on continental principles and meeting in due course an inevitable fate, or whether you will be a great country, an imperial country, a country where your sons, when they rise, to paramount positions will obtain not merely the esteem of their countrymen, but command the respect of the world.'

However, if it was Disraeli who helped to create the image of imperialism as one of self-sacrificing service in harsh conditions, what Lord Rosebery was later to call 'sane imperialism', it was Gladstone, rather than the Marxist historians, who first made 'imperialism' a mean word. It was the torrent of abuse he poured on the Empire, his defence of the rights of colonial peoples, that first focused attention on the less worthy effects of imperialism. For Gladstone imperialism was 'the new form of Jingoism', and he detested it. He condemned colonial annexations as an interference with the rights of free peoples, and he saw an expanding empire draining away the wealth and manhood of Britain in pointless wars against primitive peoples who had the right to seek their own salvation. Furthermore he believed that imperial expansion would merely provide opportunities for trouble, for 'with a great Empire in each of the four quarters of the world, and with the whole new or fifth quarter to ourselves, we may be territorially content but less than ever at our ease; for if agitator and alarmist can now find at almost every spot "British interests" to bewilder and disquiet us, their quest will then be all the wider, in proportion as the excepted points will be the fewer'.

Gladstone and his Liberal followers seemed to accept the view of Cobden that 'Our dependencies are supported at an expense in direct taxation of more than five millions annually. They serve not as gorgeous and ponderous appendages to swell our ostensible grandeur but, in reality, to complicate and magnify our government expenditure without improving our balance of trade'. But it would be wrong to overstate Disraeli's support for an expanding Empire. Disraeli spoke in terms of upholding and maintaining the Empire, of protecting it from disintegration, rather than of expansion. This defensive attitude was in fact very similar to Gladstone's view, and was indeed the essence of British foreign and imperial policy.

Disraeli's political ideals and policies were the product of a rich imagination, applied both in his novels and in his premiership. It has been argued that when he was Prime Minister this imagination was seduced by imperial fancies away from the practical realities of social reform. Perhaps rather it was the reluctance of the romantic and the dilettante to leave the languid mystical plateau of imaginative enterprise for the baser realms of legislative action. Certainly Disraeli seemed to lack the energy and the ability to deal with details which Gladstone possessed. Yet often Gladstone's energy swept all before it without careful consideration of political limitations. His policies tended to be the result of volcanic eruptions in his mind, what Magnus calls 'seismic spasms'. Usually the eruption provided Gladstone with enough conviction and determination to convert the electorate rapidly to his views. At the same time, to many his self-assured righteousness seemed to be an evasion of realities. There was also the danger that Gladstone's decisions quickly ossified, sometimes into priggishness. This may explain his abandonment of the Irish leader Parnell when revealed as an adulterer, and certainly explains Gladstone's reversal of his decision to contribute to a statue to the philosopher John Stuart Mill, whom he admired, when he learnt that Mill had at one time supported birth control.

It is possible to admire Gladstone for his integrity and the application of moral principles to politics, to condemn him as a bigot, or to examine his policies simply in the light of cause and effect and accept him as a politician. One can praise Disraeli for his realisation of the needs of his time and his defence of traditional British values, despise him for chasing after romantic illusions, or examine his policies also in an effort to assess his contribution to politics. The problem posed for the historian by the careers of Gladstone and Disraeli is not whether either was ultimately right, nor whether one was a better statesman than the other, for such decisions will depend on value judgements which may well be irreconcilable one with another. Rather it is, more simply, to examine what each contributed to the development of events in his own unique way.

Chapter II

Apprenticeship to politics 1846-1868

Before the events of 1846 it was possible that Gladstone and Disraeli could eventually have been colleagues, but it became increasingly clear after 1846 that they never would sit on the same Treasury Bench. This incompatibility was based not only on personal antipathy but also on an increasing conflict over policy which became apparent in the years before 1868. The problems of the exact content of Gladstonian Liberalism and the extent to which Disraeli was the first Tory democrat cannot be solved merely by a survey of events after 1868. Both Gladstone as Chancellor of the Exchequer, and Disraeli as Leader of the House of Commons which passed the 1867 Reform Bill, had made considerable contributions to the development of national life which would have assured them a place in history without taking into account their more illustrious roles as Prime Ministers.

1 Disraeli and the Derbyites   As Prime Minister, Disraeli emerged as an exponent of imperialism and social reform, the supposed creator of Tory democracy and a new Conservatism. The question arises whether this was mere expediency, as the only viable alternative to Gladstone's policies, or whether Disraeli held a genuine political creed which developed from the embryonic beginnings which can be seen in his early career.

Disraeli's connection with 'Young England' was perhaps the first link in a long chain. When he joined the movement in 1842 he cut an odd figure among its aristocratic founder members.

Disraeli was nearly twenty years older than his companions, hardly young and certainly not aristocratic. But he was accepted.

'Young England' was founded in the romantic Cavalier and Jacobite tradition, tempered by the medievalism of Scott's novels, by George Smythe, eldest son of Lord Strangford, and Lord John Manners, second son of the Duke of Rutland. Besides their friendship at Eton and Cambridge, Smythe and Manners shared an emotional revulsion against the liberal utilitarian spirit of the time, and they thought they saw in the willing Disraeli a kindred spirit. They resuscitated, as Robert Blake, Disraeli's biographer, has indicated, the ideal of 'a mythical, benevolent feudal system to set against the radical, centralising Benthamism which seemed to be carrying all before it in the 1830s and 1840s'. This band of knights made much of Chartist and Irish discontent, attracting more attention by the extravagance of their remarks than their numbers or ideas deserved. However, they quarrelled over the Maynooth Grant, which Disraeli opposed but Smythe and Manners supported, and the movement disintegrated.

Woodward in his book *The Age of Reform* assumes that Disraeli joined the young aristocrats because 'they provided him with a platform from which he could attack Peel, and their assistance saved him from isolation in disloyalty'. Yet Disraeli's interest in the much quoted 'two nations' of rich and poor seems quite genuine and permanent. It is reflected not only in his later advocacy of social reform but also in his three novels of the 1840s, *Coningsby, Tancred* and in particular *Sybil*. In these novels Disraeli described the social problem of England as resulting from a wicked combination of a greedy Whig landed oligarchy and unscrupulous capitalist factory owners against the helpless multitude. Under the influence of 'Young England', he offered an escape from the disagreeable present of the hardfaced mill owners and the slavery of profit to an agreeable, but imaginary, reconstruction of the past, in which the lords of the manor would once again dispense the paternal justice of a feudal society.

Disraeli and his 'Young England' companions showed a genuine concern for the benevolent working of the Poor Law, an open sympathy with Chartism, and some knowledge of the actual living conditions of the factory worker, whilst other professedly radical politicians seemed obsessed by the economics of the Corn Laws rather than the practical realities of the 1840s. Disraeli's conception was romantic and not always coherently explained, but he tenaciously clung to it, and when the opportunity came in 1874 it was possible to see the promise of 'Young England' in some respects become reality.

Usually Disraeli rather than Derby is credited with holding together the Derbyite Conservatives through the lean years after they had turned their backs on Peel. No one would deny Disraeli some of the credit, but his title to it needs examination.

Disraeli's accession to the leadership of the Protectionists or Derbyites in the House of Commons in 1849 after the death of Bentinck seems to have been inevitable. Stanley, later the four-teenth Earl of Derby, leading the faction from a seat in the Lords, and some of the hierarchy of the party, tried to avoid the distasteful appointment of a Jew and literary fop. But Disraeli's abilities outshone all others, and he made it clear that he would not accept second place in the House of Commons. Disraeli had pulled off his coup, but Stanley had not abandoned his ultimate control, as the success of his opposition to the abandonment of protection illustrated; Disraeli had to wait for Stanley's conversion.

Disraeli's objective as leader of the opposition in the Commons was to create a credible government on a Tory base to replace the coalitions on a Whig base which had followed the fall of Peel. To achieve this he needed to broaden the Church of England and gentry foundations of the party, and reverse the direction in which he had helped to lead the party since 1846. His first task, therefore, as leader of the rank and file Protectionists was to win them away from that policy. The Anti-Corn Law League had done its work well; there was no possibility of a majority in Parliament for protection. Stanley's stubborn resistance made matters more difficult for Disraeli, but he was able to note, when Stanley failed to form a government in February 1851, that 'every public man of experience and influence, however slight, had declined to act unless the principle of Protection was unequivocally renounced'. By February 1852 when Stanley, now Lord Derby, accepted office, he had agreed to abandon what Disraeli called 'the narrow defile of protection'. Disraeli's had been the voice of persuasion, but Derby's was the voice of decision. Thus the Protectionists became Derbyites, at last surrendering to political reality.

Derby's government of 1852, however, was weak in names and ability, and this remained an inherent disadvantage through 1858 and 1867 when Derby formed his second and third ministries. Not until 1874 were the Conservatives able to produce a front bench of able and distinguished ministers. It is not surprising that in these circumstances Derby and Disraeli made a principle of expediency, and that this too survived. Despite its weaknesses the Derbyite group did not disintegrate; it survived to become a brilliant opposition during Gladstone's first ministry, and eventually to form its own majority government. This was the result of the combined efforts of Disraeli and Derby. The latter lacks a full-scale historical biography, and he tends too often to appear in the shadow of his more extrovert colleague in the Commons. The Conservative party's survival was in fact due to the merits of both men. Derby's social and aristocratic position was tempered by a concern for moderate reform, which he had revealed as a leading member of the first great Whig ministry of the 1830s. To this Disraeli added ambition and brains. It was Derby who dominated the party and the governments which he headed. He needed Disraeli's flair and debating ability, but equally Disraeli needed his leader's support to bolster his shaky position in the party. Together they were able to guarantee the future of Conservatism.

When Palmerston refused to join Derby's government of 1852 as Chancellor of the Exchequer the position was offered to Disraeli, and he accepted. The situation was not promising, and the government survived only because the Peelites were prepared to co-operate until a general election in the summer in order that the estimates and the Mutiny Bill could be passed. This meant that Disraeli's April budget was merely an interim measure, and that he had until the meeting of Parliament in November finally to win Derby over to free trade. Derby agreed to the need to abandon protection, but he made no public declaration before the election. The government resumed in November and Disraeli brought forward his first real budget. He had promised compensation to those who had suffered from free trade, the landed, sugar and shipping interests, yet he did not want to unite the opposition against the government. The rise of Louis Napoleon to power in France prompted a war scare which would also mean meeting the increased demands of the armed services.

Disraeli in his 1852 budget accepted the increased service estimates, reduced the malt tax to help the landowners, reduced shipping dues and allowed the sugar manufacturers to refine in bond, instead of paying the tax on the greater volume of raw sugar. For 'the people' he reduced the tea duty. In order to pay for these concessions he proposed to lower the exemption from income tax from £150 to £100 and to extend the tax to Ireland. At the same time he reduced the exemption limit on the unpopular house tax from £20 to £10 rateable value. Compensation for some was to be very costly for others. Macaulay concluded: 'The plan was nothing but taking money out of the pockets of people in the towns and putting in into the pockets of growers of malt.'

The government had only been saved from defeat on the free trade issue by the intervention of Gladstone and Palmerston, the latter proposing a moderate motion for the acceptance of free trade to which the Derbyites agreed. Gladstone seemed to be hoping that if the government were allowed to make their own public statement on free trade it would be unsatisfactory to the Peelites, and they, or rather he at least, could then join the Whigs and Radicals with a clear conscience. In fact Disraeli's budget presented Gladstone with his opportunity. The latter was himself to be a most distinguished Chancellor of the Exchequer, and his attack on Disraeli's budget, which he described to his wife as 'disgusting and repulsive', was an indication of that distinction, as well as beginning the parliamentary duel which was to dominate English politics until Disraeli's death.

When the question of the admittance of the Jewish Lionel de Rothschild to the House of Commons was raised in 1847, and again when opposing Palmerston on the Don Pacifico question in 1850, Disraeli and Gladstone had been in agreement, but never again after 1852. Gladstone's successful attack on the budget ended all real possibility of a reconciliation between the Peelites and the Derbyites. Although it was not at once apparent, Disraeli was firmly rooted in the Conservative party, and Gladstone was propelled towards Liberalism.

Disraeli's budget of 1852 was defeated by 305 votes to 286. His task had been a difficult one in attempting to win new friends for the Derbyites without losing any of the old ones. But in trying to placate all interests he dispersed his compensation over too wide an area, raised new enemies, and pleased no one. If Disraeli had made possible the first Derbyite government, his budget certainly destroyed it. Gladstone's budget that followed had a comprehensiveness which Disraeli's lacked.

The new acrimony of their relationship became clearly apparent in the childish correspondence between them in 1853 over the Downing Street furniture and the Chancellor's robe. Disraeli was anxious to be reimbursed for the Downing Street furniture which Gladstone had taken over from him. Gladstone refused at first and demanded that Disraeli hand over to him the Chancellor's robe. This request Disraeli refused, for he believed the robe had belonged to the Younger Pitt, and he would not part with it. In the end Gladstone gave in over both the robe and the furniture, but not before the two men had descended to writing to each other in the third person.

When he was again Chancellor of the Exchequer in Derby's second ministry in 1858-9, Disraeli had little chance to make his mark on the nation's financial policy. His first budget at that time was virtually framed for him, and the government fell before he produced his second.

2 Gladstone and the road to Liberalism   Gladstone began his political career as a Tory defender of the pre-1832 constitution. He ended it by challenging the House of Lords. In the process he helped to form a great political party that became very closely identified with his own personality. It is necessary to examine how he evolved from his early Toryism to make his unique contribution to Liberalism.

Disraeli's objection to Liberalism as a foreign plant alien to English soil was in part a fair comment. The doctrines of Liberalism—the belief in progress, in equality of opportunity, in the goal of manhood suffrage and in the notion that grievances could be redressed by rational methods—had developed more dramatically in Europe and especially in France. On the other hand the empiricism of the seventeenth-century English philosopher Locke had contributed to the development of European Liberalism, and there was much in the English Utilitarian movement that was to lend itself to the new radicalism of the British Liberal party. Nonetheless it was on the Continent that the contrast between 'Liberalism' and 'autocracy' could be seen sharp and clear, and it was through his visits to the Continent that Gladstone perceived the road he was to tread.

On his visit to Naples in 1850-1 the political trials and the condition of political prisoners provided a sharp jolt to Gladstone's stern conscience. The result was his pamphlet *A Letter to Lord Aberdeen*, which won for him not only the congratulations of Palmerston but also the admiration of many British and European liberals with a faith in constitutional government. In Naples Gladstone came to the conclusion that about twenty thousand political prisoners were languishing in conditions of filth and cruelty: 'It is the wholesale persecution of virtue . . . It is the awful profanation of public religion . . . It is the perfect prostitution of the judicial office . . . It is the savage and cowardly system of moral as well as physical torture . . . This is the negation of God erected into a system of government.'

Hammond in his *Gladstone and the Irish Nation* has pointed out also the importance of an earlier visit to the Continent to meet Guizot in 1845. It was then that Gladstone first heard Europe's opinions of England's treatment of Ireland, opinions which Gladstone was later to accept. Other significant visits to the Continent were to follow.

Gladstone's interpretation of Liberalism sprang from his deep religious convictions. In it he found the nearest approach, in a political philosophy, to what he regarded as the will of God. In a more secular age, when the religious convictions of our politicians do not appear to be basic to their political philosophy, Gladstone's religious beliefs may appear rather odd, but in the nineteenth century they were the beacon which led the people to him. Gladstone's attempt to raise the moral standards and ideals of the people became the basis of his own brand of Liberalism.

Gladstone appreciated the vital importance to the success of his mission of the need to improve the material conditions of the people, but he believed that this must come from the individual's own thrift and industry, rather than through state intervention. The state's duty was to provide the right environment by creating opportunities for individuals to help themselves, and to make sure that those already enjoying advantages did not abuse them at the expense of the majority. He wished to avoid the situation where some people became parasites living off a welfare state. Gladstone did not object to the financial cost of such a venture in itself, but to the fact that social parasites have lost the self-respect without which they cannot be moral individuals. Gladstone was not parsimonious, but he condemned extravagance as a great social and moral evil. He did not adopt a policy of laissez-faire, but rather sought to reduce prices, secure full employment, and keep public expenditure and taxation to a minimum. He believed that all but the poorest should contribute to taxation, for this too would create self-respect and make the individual more aware of his rôle as a member of the community. These views were reflected in Gladstone's budgets, which thus illustrate an essential aspect of Gladstonian Liberalism.

3 Gladstone as Chancellor of the Exchequer Gladstone's budgets in the 1850s and 1860s sought to extend commerce by the advocacy of free trade, for he saw such a policy assisting the nation's wealth to 'fructify in the pockets of the people'. At the same time he planned to reduce and eventually abolish the income tax, but war and fear of war always intruded. The continuation of income tax became for him not only a financial necessity but also a punishment. No other Chancellor would have seen the hand of God in an increase in taxation. In 1854, when he doubled the tax to 1s 2d in the pound to help pay for the Crimean War, he declared, 'The expenses of war are a moral check, which it has pleased the Almighty to impose upon the ambition and the lust of conquest that are inherent in so many nations.'

Gladstone's first budget of 1853, when he was a member of the Peelite-Whig coalition under Lord Aberdeen, epitomises his method and his financial ideals. In contrast to Disraeli's efforts of 1852, the budget of 1853 embodied a coherent plan with a precise purpose.

Gladstone planned to retain income tax at 7d in the pound for two years, reducing it gradually and dispensing with it in 1860. Peel had temporarily reintroduced the tax in order to attack tariffs, and that too was Gladstone's motive in retaining it. Duties were removed from 123 articles, mainly manufactured goods, and reduced on a further 133. The Anti-Corn Law League had long pressed that the people should enjoy a 'free breakfast table', and in lowering duties mainly on fruits and dairy produce Gladstone was fulfilling their policy.

The Crimean War put an end to Gladstone's optimism, whilst his antipathy to Palmerston kept him out of office. From 1859 to 1865, however, he was again Chancellor of the Exchequer in the Palmerston-Russell coalition.

The 1860 budget, in leaving only 48 articles on the tariff, completed for all practical purposes the policy of free trade, and though income tax was retained at 10d this was largely to help pay for a military expedition to China and the provision of iron-clads for the navy. Gladstone found that he could not do without income tax, but he sought to adjust the rate at which it was levied. Thus in 1864 the tax was reduced to 5d and in 1865 to 4d. Yet at the same time it was possible for Gladstone to reduce further the customs duties; in 1864 the duty on sugar was lowered, and in 1865 the duty on tea reduced from 1s to 6d. The timber duty, which Gladstone had long opposed, was finally removed in 1866.

Gladstone was always anxious to reduce government expenditure, the source of his disagreements with Palmerston, and in this he was concerned with minor details as well as with vast sums. One of his first actions as Chancellor was to compel the Foreign Office to abandon its practice of using large thick sheets of double note-paper, when single, thinner sheets would suffice. He included himself in this economy drive. Whenever in office he used the same notepaper for his private as for his official correspondence, but insisted on paying for all the notepaper which he used for any purpose which was not in the strictest sense official.

As G. M. Young in his *Portrait of an Age* has pointed out, Gladstone's budgets 'swing majestically down the tideway of an unexampled prosperity'. In 1863 Gladstone announced a twenty per cent increase in the national income between 1856 and 1861. In 1866 government expenditure stood at £66 million, having been over £70 million in 1860. In such material prosperity and low taxation Gladstone saw the salvation of the masses.

There seems little doubt that free trade was a stimulus to the British economy, but Gladstone and others may well have over-estimated its importance, ignoring the impact of improvements in communications by rail and steamship. The wisdom of continuing a policy of free trade after 1870, following the agricultural depression and the resurgence of protectionist policies in Europe, is still a matter of dispute amongst economists. Even so the absolute increase in Britain's foreign trade in the years 1870-89 was greater than that of either the United States or Germany, her two main rivals. Furthermore, economic considerations were only one part of Gladstone's policy. Influenced by Cobden, he also appreciated the political benefits of a policy which was based on co-operation between nations rather than the competitive instincts of mercantilism.

As a Chancellor of the Exchequer who had reduced both direct and indirect taxation for three successive years, Gladstone not only increased his own stature as a popular politician, but was also a valuable source of strength to a government which, ironically, since it had been based on Palmerston's reputation, found itself under heavy attack for its foreign policy. Palmerston before he died had prophesied to Shaftesbury, 'Gladstone will soon have it all his own way, and, whenever he gets my place, we shall have strange doings.'

4 Gladstone and Palmerston Gladstone's relationship with Palmerston taught him an important political lesson—the need to temper his moral conscience according to the political realities of the nineteenth century. Gladstone was to emerge from his struggles with Palmerston, the leader of the Liberal party, not perhaps a better man, but certainly a better politician. Just as Disraeli's Jewish and literary background was an obstacle to real political power which he had to overcome, so too was Gladstone's pious morality an obstacle to the fulfilment of his political career. Furthermore, like Disraeli, Gladstone found it necessary to learn the political art of compromise. Both acquired this art, as shown by their attitudes to reform in 1867 and to the question of the leadership of their respective parties before they became Prime Minister. Disraeli learnt his lesson over the issue of protection and the long years of enforced opposition, whilst Gladstone benefited from the need to come to terms with Palmerston. That Gladstone perhaps found political tactics more distasteful than Disraeli should not blind us to the fact that he too became proficient in them.

Gladstone had agreed to the Crimean War because he saw it as an attempt to make Russia obey the public law of Europe, but when Palmerston became Prime Minister Gladstone resigned. He believed that Palmerston sought to continue the war unnecessarily, and he was affronted by the Committee of Inquiry into the war. The press, which had praised him for his 1853 budget, now criticised him as a pious fanatic. His attack on Palmerston's Chinese policy seemed to push him further into the political void, for no ministry without Palmerston seemed capable of survival in the aimless politics of the mid-century. In an age dominated by foreign policy Gladstone had unusual and unpopular views. Even his sojourn in 1858-9 as Lord High Commissioner Extraordinary to the Ionian Islands, where he attempted to reconcile the islanders to continued British rule, failed to deflect Gladstone from the path he believed God had chosen for him as a politician. In 1858 that path was still blocked by the jingoistic figure of Palmerston. Nevertheless by the end of 1859 Gladstone was back in the main stream of English political life.

Derby's ministry of 1858-9 preferred to ignore Italy's demand for rejuvenation by means of unification and constitutional, democratic government. However, it was this issue which provided a bridge between Gladstone's liberal sympathies and Palmerston's Whig version of foreign policy. Gladstone became Palmerston's Chancellor of the Exchequer.

Gladstone had met Cavour in March 1859 when returning from the Ionian Islands and had become converted to the view that the problems of Italy were as much due to Austrian rule as to Neapolitan backwardness. Morley in his biography of Gladstone insists that 'the dilemma between joining Derby and joining Palmerston was no vital choice between political creeds'. At a time when the establishment of a government depended more on personal accidents than on large views of policy, there was little to chose between Derby and Palmerston on domestic matters. Yet the question of the liberation of Italy raised an issue similar to that of the Spanish Civil War in the 1930s or that of Vietnam in the 1960s, and drew men by their sympathies into more definite political alignments. Gladstone joined Palmerston because the Conservatives seemed to be in sympathy with the Austrians. Even in 1864 Disraeli refused to meet Garibaldi during his visit to England. Gladstone himself later wrote to Lord Acton: 'The overwhelming interest and welfare of the Italian question, and of our foreign policy in connection with it, joined to my entire mistrust of the former government in relation to it, led me to decide without a moment's hesitation.'

Gladstone's support for Italy goes back to the first half of the decade, and the decision to join Palmerston's government was not a landmark on the road to Liberalism. It was, however, a most vital step in Gladstone's career for two reasons. Firstly, in Derby's government Gladstone was probably aware that he would have been one young man amongst many, whereas with the aged Palmerston and Russell there was a good possibility that he would emerge as their natural successor. Gladstone in 1858 had said to Graham, one of his old Peelite colleagues, that no worse minister than Palmerston had held office in their time. However it is difficult to avoid the conclusion that in choosing to join Palmerston Gladstone was not rejecting Derby, though he was rejecting possible subservience to Disraeli as leader of the Derbyites in the House of Commons. His enthusiasm for Italy provided a convenient door to shut on his old party. Secondly it was a vital decision because in Palmerston's and Russell's cabinets Gladstone was to contact the remnants of the moderate Whigs, whilst his advocacy of parliamentary reform in 1864 was to win over to him Radicals such as Bright and John Stuart Mill. From the welding together of these two political elements Gladstone was to create his first ministry.

No sooner had he joined Palmerston's cabinet in 1859 than the Prime Minister's concern for the state of Britain's defences and Gladstone's frugality in government expenditure led to disputes. The war scare of 1859-60 following Napoleon III's annexation of Nice and Savoy, and French interest in building the Suez Canal, which Cobden described as the greatest public delusion since the days of Titus Oates, may have affected Palmerston, but not Gladstone, who saw economic ties as an antidote to war.

Cobden had originally canvassed the idea of a commercial treaty with France as early as 1849, and in 1859 he tried again. Naturally he consulted the Chancellor of the Exchequer, and Gladstone was encouraging, for he saw a chance to complete Peel's work, agreeing also with Cobden that the treaty would reduce tension between the two countries.

Cobden's Commercial Treaty with France in 1860 lay partly behind the tariff charges of the 1860 budget, but at first it was not clear the tariff charges would be passed. The Cabinet, led by Palmerston, was not convinced of the value of the alliance with France, the increased income tax seemed offensive, and English manufacturers were concerned about French competition. Gladstone, however, regarded the commercial treaty and his budget that went with it as a great European operation, and he convinced the House of Commons and the country of its rightness. He explained that France was to receive nothing which Britain would benefit from keeping, and that 'at a small loss of revenue we had gained a great extension of trade'. Grenville was of the opinion that Gladstone 'achieved one of the greatest triumphs that the House of Commons ever witnessed'.

The disagreement between the Prime Minister and his Chancellor was further complicated by the report of a Commission issued in 1859 which recommended the spending of £11 million on coastal fortifications. This Gladstone would not agree to. In addition the budget of 1860 had attempted to abolish the excise duty on paper at a cost of over £1 million. Palmerston objected to this. He wished the money to be used for national defence, and he was even to tell the Queen that the House of Lords would do good service in rejecting the proposition. The Lords did reject the Bill, and though Gladstone was anxious to fight them he gave way as neither Palmerston nor the rest of the Cabinet were prepared to support him. He also compromised over the question of fortifications, for Palmerston insisted that 'our colonies, our commerce and the subsistence of a large part of our population would be at the mercy of our enemy'. The fortifications were paid for largely by raising a loan, but there was also an increase in income tax, partly as Gladstone's punishment for the warmongers who insisted on increases in military and naval expenditure. Thus 'Palmerston's follies' first appeared in the landscape of southern England.

Palmerston and Gladstone continued to quarrel over fortifications, and on three occasions the latter threatened to resign. He remained in office, as he explained to Cobden, because he felt that he could still exercise his influence in favour of moderation in expenditure. Gladstone may also have felt that one more temperamental resignation would ruin his political career.

Gladstone did have his own way over the excise duty on paper in 1861 by putting all his financial proposals in one Bill, and defying the Lords to reject the entire budget. Palmerston disapproved of Gladstone's methods, but the Lords passed the first finance Bill by a majority of fifteen.

The programme of fortification and naval construction was under way, and after 1861 the two men learnt to live with each other until Gladstone's statement on parliamentary reform in 1864. Gladstone never accepted Palmerston's bellicose attitude to foreign policy, nor did he agree with Palmerston that in domestic matters 'there is really nothing to be done . . . we cannot go on adding to the Statute Book ad infinitum . . . we cannot go on legislating for ever'. By the time of Palmerston's death in 1865 Gladstone had moved from the economic radicalism of Cobden to the political radicalism of Bright. What is more important is that Gladstone had learnt the political value of such a move.

5 Gladstone, Disraeli and parliamentary reform A central issue in an assessment of the early careers of Gladstone and Disraeli is their attitudes to parliamentary reform. Did they both accept the need for a radical reform of the franchise, or was Gladstone merely hoping to include the sober and respectable of the lower class, and Disraeli merely seeking political advantage? Which of them deserves the credit for the 1867 Reform Act? These questions are still open to debate, but some conclusions can be drawn by investigating the motives of both men as far as this is possible, and then examining the developments of 1866-7.

Gladstone's attitude to reform is the more difficult to disentangle. In May 1864 he astonished the House of Commons by making his famous declaration on reform: 'I venture to say that every man who is not presumably incapacitated by some consideration of personal unfitness or of political danger, is morally entitled to come within the pale of the constitution.' Gladstone went on to make clear that he was opposed to 'sudden, or violent, or excessive, or intoxicating change'; but it was the first sentence that was remembered. Even when the whole speech was published later with an explanatory preface, it remained clear to Palmerston, who protested strongly on behalf of 'all persons who value the maintenance of our institutions', if not to Gladstone, that he had in fact advocated manhood suffrage. Gladstone had clearly escaped from the heritage of 1830, though his popular reputation seems to have been slightly in advance of his actual thinking.

Parliamentary reform, however, was not an issue in the election of July 1865, and it was a parliament sympathetic to Palmerston which met. It was the death of Palmerston in October 1865 which put an altogether different complexion on events. Bright had already commented in 1862, 'As for Palmerston, he is the last link connecting us with a past generation, and when his time is out, we shall enter on a new and I believe a better time.' Disraeli too commented on new developments in political life: 'The truce of parties is over. I foresee tempestuous times, and great vicissitudes in public life.' Robert Lowe, the intellectual opponent of reform, saw clearly the writing on the wall, for he believed the rest of the government 'by way of a mortuary contribution, to have buried in his grave all their prudence, statesmanship and moderation'. Lord John Russell, who had introduced the 1832 Reform Bill, became Prime Minister, and a reform Bill was introduced in March 1866.

Russell's and Gladstone's Reform Bill of 1866 was a moderate measure, merely seeking to reduce the borough franchise from £10 to £7, and to include in the county franchise those paying an annual rent of at least £4. There was even a fancy franchise for those who had £50 or more in a savings bank over a period of two years, though it was not to be a qualification for a double vote. The accompanying Redistribution Bill, rather than abolishing the smaller boroughs, attempted instead to group some of them together into larger constituencies. The aim was clearly a 'mixed' rather than a democratic constitution, though this did not prevent Disraeli from declaring that the reduction of the franchise would produce a parliament consisting of 'a horde of selfish and obscure mediocrities, incapable of anything but mischief, and that mischief devised and regulated by the raging demagogue of the hour'.

However, what led to the government's resignation was not the opposition of the Conservatives, but the rebellion within the Liberal Party of Robert Lowe and those whom Bright called the Adullamites after the inhabitants of a dark biblical cave.

Lowe's objection was not that of a mere reactionary; he objected to the further enfranchisement of the masses not out of love of aristocracy but out of a fear of the ignorance of the lower orders in society. His fear was that politics would be at the mercy of the mass organisation of passive working men by corrupt party bosses as had happened in the United States. He rejected Gladstone's thesis that many of the labouring classes had 'earned' the right to vote, and he did not accept the 'inevitability' of reform, which in the minds of some was justified by Darwin's theory of evolution.

Despite the defeat of the government Gladstone carried on the fight for reform from the opposition benches, and indeed is often credited with the real responsibility for the details of the 1867 Bill. This raises the question of whether Gladstone was moved by a revelation from God which he could not contain, whether his previous political experience had convinced him of the need for reform, or whether he was simply flying a kite to see which way the wind was blowing. Recent research, such as that of Maurice Cowling in his study of the 1867 Reform Act, and that of John Vincent into the formation of the Liberal Party, is unearthing rather devious tactics beneath the surface of Gladstone's activities in the years 1864-7.

Cowling has pointed out that Liberal historians 'see Liberalism as a doctrine rather than a political party, and Radicalism as truth rather than ideology'. To Morley and G. M. Trevelyan, Gladstone was the personification of this Liberal image—a Moses leading the people progressively towards a new life. Philip Magnus in his biography of Gladstone first drew attention to the sudden, rather than evolutionary, development of Gladstone's views, the 'volcanic eruptions' of his mind. More recent research indicates a different and perhaps more realistic image of Gladstone—the man as a politician. This is clearly seen in Gladstone's relationship with Bright and in his ambiguous position over parliamentary reform.

After Gladstone's speech of 1864 in favour of franchise reform, he and Bright drew together, and they were in close touch before the 1865 election, though Bright was not consulted about the

1866 Bill, and Gladstone viewed with alarm Bright's idea of household suffrage in the boroughs. At the same time Gladstone was rejected by Oxford University and elected by the more populous S.E. Lancashire constituency in the 1865 election. He was coming down to the people as a political leader. As a squire on his Hawarden estate he had earlier provided relief work for those unemployed in the cotton famine occasioned by the American Civil War. The effect on him of the suffering of the cotton operatives remained with him on his tour of the North-East, when he found himself hailed for the first time as a hero of the masses.

During the reform agitation of 1866-7, when Gladstone withdrew to Italy, it was Bright in his public speeches who built up Gladstone's reputation as leader of the Liberal Party, following Russell's resignation. As Vincent remarks: 'The Liberal Party would have remained essentially Whig and Palmerstonian without Bright, as Gladstone's bulldog, holding together the Nonconformist and working class interests outside parliament, in a broad-bottomed Radicalism.' Donald Read in his study of Cobden and Bright has come to much the same conclusion: 'Bright, as much as Gladstone, created the Gladstonian Liberal Party.'

Many of the leading Liberals such as Bright and J. S. Mill first made their political reputations outside Parliament. Once they had built up goodwill it was apparently easy for Gladstone to appear on the scene and steal their thunder. In this way the parliamentary Liberals, working-class reformers and middle-class Nonconformists were united under Gladstone. The men and events which influenced Gladstone in this critical period of his career have been frequently chronicled, but what is more difficult to estimate is the effect on Gladstone's way of thinking created by the popular audiences which from 1865 became increasingly responsive to him. G. Kitson Clark in *The Making of Victorian England* believes this helps to account for Gladstone's becoming 'a renegade from the educated classes'.

Gladstone used Bright, just as he used the demand for parliamentary reform, to secure the leadership of the Liberal party, and yet managed to retain the support, grudging though it might be, of most Whigs. Gladstone and Russell in 1866 attempted to keep the Liberal party together by a moderate approach in an attempt to please everyone. The Adullamite Cave, however, did not trust Gladstone's moderation, and it was their rebellion that led Gladstone to a more democratic position. Such a position was not of his choosing, and the Bill of 1866 was clearly an exclusion Bill. Gladstone's reform speech of 1864 enabled him to appeal to the radical faction of the party, whilst the Bill of 1866, with its clear opposition to household suffrage, enabled him to appeal to the right and centre. Gladstone seems to have been more aware of practical political realities than some of his biographers tend to give him credit for. Cowling clearly sees in Gladstone's speeches and letters of the period 'a tortuous, powerful and casuistical attempt to keep all options open'. Such a remark Morley would have found impossible to make.

Disraeli's motives are perhaps more easy to determine, but his tactics were no less devious. Until 1852 the two main parties had an unwritten agreement not to broach the subject of parliamentary reform, though in 1848 Disraeli had pointed out that his party was as much entitled as any other to reconstruct the estate of the Commons when the time was ripe. Neither Disraeli nor Derby felt that the Conservatives should keep to a settlement which, as it was made by their opponents, was clearly designed to operate against their interests. It was Russell in 1852 and again in 1854 who attempted unsuccessfully to break the deadlock on reform. Even Palmerston in 1857 claimed that he intended to deal with the problem of reform quite soon. It was therefore quite natural for Derby to announce in 1859 that part of his programme would involve the reform of Parliament, especially as his son was an enthusiast.

The Reform Bill of 1859 was not a success. The measure proposed to reduce the £50 franchise in the counties to the borough figure of £10, to redistribute fifteen seats in favour of large unrepresented towns in thickly populated country areas, and to deprive certain freeholders in the boroughs of their right to vote in the county constituencies. Although documentary evidence is lacking, it is likely that Disraeli was responsible for the additional franchises, which Bright ridiculed as the 'fancy franchises'. These conferred votes on those who had an income of £10 per annum from government investments, on possessors of £60 in a savings bank, and on persons receiving government pensions over £20 per annum, as well as on doctors, lawyers, university graduates, ministers of religion, and certain distinguished categories of schoolmasters. Apart from the fancy franchises the Radicals objected to the Bill's failure to alter the borough franchise, and, though Gladstone supported the Bill, the rest of the opposition saw it for what it was—an attempt to strengthen the Conservatives at the expense of the rest. It was defeated in the House of Commons by thirty-nine votes. However, Disraeli had learnt one important lesson: although the Bill had been too liberal to please many Tories, it had also been too conservative to win over the Radicals and secure a majority.

On Russell's resignation in 1866 another opportunity presented itself to the Tories. Lowe, as leader of the Adullamites, seemed prepared to work with the Conservatives in opposing further reform, though he was not prepared to join with Derby and Disraeli, as some of the reactionary Tories hoped. Disraeli was anxious to pursue both a party and a personal line. He wanted to broaden the party, but at the same time to strengthen his position within it. From a party point of view the obvious thing to do was to win over a Whig contingent, but this could well bring in rivals to Disraeli's personal position in the party. Disraeli was, therefore, anxious to keep the Adullamites at arm's length, and sought to make the party a credible instrument of safe and sensible government. Derby had come to much the same conclusion, and rejected any thought of a coalition with the Adullamites. He was not troubled, however, by personal considerations, and seems to have been genuinely concerned with seizing the initiative and the credit for reform.

Robert Blake, by drawing on the correspondence of Derby and Disraeli, has effectively dispelled the view that the idea for a reform Bill in 1867 owed much to Disraeli. The latter in fact was mainly concerned to postpone legislation as long as possible. Thus the image of a zealous reformer that Disraeli cleverly propagated and that Buckle has perpetuated for him, has been dimmed. But once Derby had decided to introduce reform, Disraeli pursued the idea, determined in his old purpose of keeping the Conservative party in office by securing for it the popularity of a reforming ministry. Thus he rejected the Queen's proposal that the matter should be settled on a non-party basis in the Privy Council, and published a book containing his own speeches on parliamentary reform in an effort to prove his party's long-term interest in the matter.

Disraeli's intention was to move at a leisurely pace and introduce legislation in 1868, but in February 1867, without authority from the Cabinet, Disraeli in a parliamentary debate pledged the government to an immediate Bill. Pressure was building up from all directions, and Disraeli was concerned lest Gladstone and the Liberals should introduce a new measure. Disraeli was suddenly faced with the task of framing a Bill that would satisfy the Commons, and yet maintain Cabinet solidarity by preventing the resignations of the cautious Cranborne, Carnarvon and General Peel. The Cabinet put aside their idea of introducing plural voting, and accepted the 'Ten Minutes Bill'—just ten minutes before Derby left to attend a party meeting.

The Bill was introduced into the House of Commons that same afternoon. It kept a high £6 rating franchise in the boroughs and £20 in the counties and fancy franchises, but no plurality. There was an uproar in the House when the Bill was read. The demand for household suffrage had gathered considerable support even amongst the back-benchers, and a few days later, on 26th February, Disraeli promised to bring in a reconsidered Bill. Derby and Disraeli decided to revert to a fairly radical measure, despite opposition within the Cabinet, because they were aware that a compromise measure would be torn to pieces by Gladstone and lead to a humiliating resignation. Peel, Cranborne and Carnarvon resigned. Derby had decided to appeal to the parliamentary party against opposition in the Cabinet, holding out the threat of Gladstone waiting in the wings.

Disraeli was not a democrat, as the original drafts of the 1859 and 1867 Bills make clear. He sought to acquire popular favour without introducing a popular measure. He did not exclude household suffrage, he simply attempted to avoid it. He did not change his mind during the passage of the Bill, but he had learnt the lesson of his failure in 1859, and gave way to the majority. By 1867 ignominious opposition had made Disraeli, and many other Conservatives, take the risk of household suffrage. The prospect of power enabled them to overcome their fears.

The intention of Disraeli's Bill, introduced on 18 March 1867, was to increase the representation of the labouring classes by basing the franchise in the boroughs on personal payment of rates, and by reducing the county franchise to £15 per annum rental. It was not his intention, however, to give the labouring classes a majority, for to allow one class to predominate would be contrary to the constitution. This defence of the constitution was to be accomplished in two ways. In the first place there was to be no extensive redistribution of seats—just fifteen to the counties, only fourteen to the boroughs, and one to the University of London. Secondly a number of checks and balances were proposed, such as the residential qualification of two years, and the exclusion of compound ratepayers—those who, like many modern council tenants, paid their rates along with the weekly rent. The main balance was the allocation of the dual vote to university graduates, members of the learned professions, those who paid one pound or more per annum in direct taxation, and those with £50 in government funds, the Bank of England, or a savings bank. The fancy franchises had reappeared, slightly modified, and now carrying the right to a second vote.

However, the Bill which was passed in the House of Commons on 15 August 1867 abandoned the fancy franchises, lowered the residential qualifications to one year, and allowed the compound ratepayer to vote. At the same time the franchise in the counties was lowered to £12, and the redistribution clauses provided for forty-five new seats by taking one member from each borough of fewer than 10,000 inhabitants. Twenty-five seats were allocated to the counties, and fifteen to the towns. A third member was provided for Liverpool, Manchester, Birmingham and Leeds, and one member for the University of London.

H. J. Hanham, in his *Elections and Party Management*, has emphasised that though some very large boroughs had been created by the Act, there were plenty of others of another sort to balance them. Furthermore the countryside was still carefully sealed off from the town, and the county franchise carefully limited so that there should be no infiltration of new voters that could undermine the country gentleman's control of the shire. Nevertheless for contemporaries the 'shooting of Niagara', 'the leap in the dark', had brought in a new era. The age of professionalised politics, of party programmes, permanent legislation and mandates was beginning to emerge.

One Conservative M.P. asked how he could accept extreme reform from a bad Jew, after having refused moderate reform from a good Christian. Disraeli had not educated his party but deceived it, yet in deceiving he saved it, for he summoned Democracy to the aid of Aristocracy. How had this turn of events come about?

Morley considered, and indeed many others have since agreed with him, that the Reform Act of 1867 was an extraordinary result: 'The great reform was carried by a parliament elected to support Lord Palmerston, and Lord Palmerston detested reform. It was carried by a government in a decided minority. It was carried by a minister and by a leader of the opposition neither of whom was at that time in the full confidence of his party. Finally it was carried by a House of Commons that the year before had, in effect, rejected a measure for the admission of only 400,000 new voters, while the measure to which it now assented added almost a million voters to the electorate.'

Whilst Morley's verdict is generally acceptable, his assumption, one made originally by Cranborne in 1868, that Gladstone as Leader of the Opposition carried the Bill, can be questioned. None of the amendments proposed personally by Gladstone was accepted, for though they would have prevented the indiscriminate enfranchisement of the borough occupiers, Disraeli and Derby preferred to accept other and more radical amendments rather than allow Gladstone, as the official representative of the Opposition and their possible successor, any credit. It was after all

Hodgkinson's amendment, not Gladstone's, that secured borough democracy. Disraeli and Derby were not concerned with passing a particular reform Bill; their intention was to pass any reform Bill which would enable them to overcome Gladstone and Russell and thus stay in power as an effective government with a secure majority. Neither of the Conservative leaders planned the events of 1867 nor wished for such a Bill as was passed in that year, but both were prepared to accept such a Bill in order to 'dish the Whigs', and thus effectively to break the Liberal monopoly of power.

The actual details of the Bill sprang spontaneously from the circumstances of the mid-sixties: the effect of Lincoln's anti-slavery victory in the American Civil War, the visit of Garibaldi the romantic democrat, the economic crisis of 1866, and the following bad winter and harvest. Again the death of Palmerston encouraged not only the parliamentary reformers such as Bright and Russell, but also revitalised the radical reform organisations in England such as the northern Reform Union, which was established in 1861 and was in many ways the heir of the Anti-Corn Law League, and the Reform League, established in 1865 with many ex-Chartists amongst its members. The 1867 Reform Act, with its gift of democracy in the boroughs, reflected more the mood outside Parliament than within. Historians tend to personalise historical events—it is difficult to avoid the temptation—but arguments about the importance of individual personalities and the causation of historical events are not the province of this book. Suffice it to say, without agreeing entirely with Tolstoy's view that the meanest private in the French army did as much to affect historical development as the great Napoleon, that personalities in history often reflect the social context in which they have their being, and are not 'gods who treat us for their sport'. The tactics of Disraeli, the concern of Gladstone, merely allowed the demand for reform to become reality. What is more certain is that after 1867 the idea of government for the people by an aristocracy was, with increasing velocity, replaced by the idea of government by the people through their elected representatives.

From the full text of his speech in 1864, from the proposals of the 1866 Reform Bill, and from the amendments such as the £6 borough franchise which he failed to achieve in 1867, it is clear that Gladstone was not a supporter of household suffrage, and favoured a more restricted Bill. It is thus difficult to accept the popular version of the 1868 election according to which the new voters, having seen through the pose of Mr. Disraeli, thanked Mr. Gladstone by returning him to office. Hanham has pointed out that the redistribution of seats did not go far enough to allow the newly enfranchised majorities their full power, whilst the qualifications for the franchise had become so complicated that it is difficult to know how many new voters were enfranchised in particular constituencies. It was after all the disestablishment of the Irish Church which provided the main national issue in the election of 1868, a matter of policy and prejudice, rather than personality. That there was some delay in getting the compounders, those paying their rates with their rent, on the electoral register may have been fatal for the Conservative party; many in the boroughs were unable to vote until 1874. However, in spite of all this it would be incorrect to assume that they then thanked Mr. Disraeli, for there were so many more issues at stake in the 1874 election than the authorship of the Reform Bill of 1867.

The Conservative myth of Disraeli as the educator of his party in 1867 no longer has enough substance to be convincing. Blake has pointed out that for 1867 all the evidence of Disraeli's papers suggests that he still thought of politics as management and influence, not in terms of the mass persuasion of a new class. Derby was right in his judgement that the 1867 Act was 'a leap in the dark', and it was only as Gladstone's first ministry progressed that the light of Tory democracy, based on imperialism and social reform, began to dawn on Disraeli. Yet his performance in 1867 was vital for Disraeli, for it dazzled the Conservative Party into accepting him as leader on Derby's resignation in 1868. This was what Disraeli wanted. As Blake concludes on Disraeli's apprenticeship, 'For what he did in 1867 he deserves to go down in history as a politician of genius, a superb improviser, a parliamentarian of unrivalled skill, but not as a far-sighted statesman, a Tory democrat, or the educator of his party.'

6 The election of 1868 The resignation of Derby in February 1868, owing to ill health, allowed Disraeli his first but brief view of politics from 'the top of the greasy pole'. Already at the end of 1867 Gladstone had succeeded Russell as leader of the Whiggish Liberal Party. Gladstone was not popular with the party. They had not co-operated with him in his efforts to amend the Conservative Reform Bill; the Whigs distrusted him for his support of reform, while the Radicals were not convinced of his conversion. However, Gladstone seized the initiative, and, when his resolution that the Church of Ireland must cease to exist as a church in alliance with the state was carried, Disraeli announced the dissolution of the House for the autumn and the holding of a general election based on the new register. It is ironic that Ireland, so often in the future to divide the Liberal Party, in 1868 brought the various elements of the party together, and even reconciled Lowe to his old colleagues.

The Conservatives hoped for victory in the election, perhaps expected a small Liberal majority, and were obviously disappointed by the Liberal majority of 112. The Conservative support of the Irish Church may have won them votes in Lancashire, but elsewhere in the great towns and among Nonconformists they lost votes. Also, of course, their traditional Roman Catholic voters did not vote for them. There was certainly little attempt by the Conservatives to appeal to the new electors with a policy of social reform, though one of the Conservative candidates in Birmingham wooed the trade unions. Whilst Disraeli was satisfied with the usual written election address to his constituents, Gladstone and Bright as the chief orators of the party undertook a country-wide campaign in which they made clear their acceptance of the implications of the Reform Act.

In his diary for his 59th birthday, shortly after assuming the position of Prime Minister, Gladstone records, 'The Almighty seems to sustain and spare me for some purpose of His own, deeply unworthy as I know myself to be. Glory be to His name.'

Chapter III

Full steam—domestic affairs 1868-86

1 A new age? With one and a half million votes cast for the Liberals as opposed to one million for the Conservatives, the 1868 election produced the first clear-cut majority in the House of Commons since 1841. In its resolute attempt to solve the problems of the time Gladstone's first administration is often regarded as the first modern government, heralding a new age. How far is this view acceptable?

Elected by the people rather than by a particular class, and convinced that the hand of God was involved, Gladstone attempted to govern for the people rather than catering merely for the interests of one class. The impact of the government's legislation can be compared to that of the Whig ministries of the 1830s and of Attlee's Labour ministry of 1945-51. 1868 saw the beginning of a period of rapid reform which had profound effects on all sections of the community. To later generations which have experienced reformist Toryism, radical Liberalism and Socialism, this opinion may seem highly exaggerated. But to the generation which had lived through the stagnation in domestic legislation of Palmerston's era, the Gladstonian interpretation of Liberalism was almost revolutionary in its effects. Even though many aspects of a hierarchical society were to survive, great steps were taken in securing equality of opportunity and even of status. Established churches were threatened, landlord privileges were eroded, and the political domination of the aristocracy was imperilled.

As G. M. Young has explained, this new Liberalism was formed 'of definite grievance and redress, Church rates and University tests, Army purchase and Irish Disestablishment, and a humane and frugal distrust of Empire, aristocracy, adventure and war'. Until 1867 the Liberal Party had been the expression of personal rivalries and political differences within the aristocratic and gentry class. After that date, however, the Liberals came to represent great and dynamic social forces in the country, in particular the radicalism of the new industrial classes. This development Gladstone achieved by linking the parliamentary party to the radicalism of the rank and file. It was the beginning of the process whereby the executive, as representative of the whole nation, began to assume responsibility for the great matters of national life, and Parliament ceased to behave solely as the representative of the gentry.

In his study of the mid-Victorian generation W. L. Burn briefly characterises the tone of the years 1852-67: 'Although there was a great deal of talk about the middle classes the government of the country was still aristocratically directed; local government was still markedly in some respects chaotically local; France rather than Prussia or Germany was the enemy to be feared; the labouring classes were still, for the most part, subordinate to their betters and their employers.' By the end of Gladstone's first ministry alone considerable inroads had been made into that simple structure. By 1874 the England of the School Boards and of popular participation in politics had definitely emerged, the purchase of commissions in the Army had ceased and the highest ranks of the Civil Service were at last recruited by open competition. Talent was beginning to count for rather more than birth or connection, and it was Gladstone's first ministry which began that quiet social revolution.

Morley tells us that Gladstone regarded his first Cabinet as 'one of the best instruments for government that was ever constructed'. G. M. Trevelyan saw in the Cabinet 'old Radicalism made presentable'; the appointments of Bright and Forster were proof that government by the old Whig families was at an end. Certainly it was the first Cabinet to represent the variety of the Liberal party, and for the first time nine Cabinet ministers sat in the House of Commons. However, important appointments for

Clarendon and Granville among others indicate that the Cabinet had its share of peers and Whigs. Furthermore, in 1880 Gladstone made even more Whig appointments, for he was anxious to maintain the unity of the party. Gladstone's policy was that the group which was weakest in the House of Commons should be strongest in the Cabinet, and in 1880 the result was that the great posts went entirely to Whigs. The only Radical in the Cabinet then, apart from Bright, was Joseph Chamberlain, and Gladstone himself had preferred the more acceptable Sir Charles Dilke, who had pressed Chamberlain in his stead.

Gladstone believed in both innovation and continuity. The problems of reform, however, heightened the differences of opinion between the factions in the party. During the first ministry Gladstone managed to ride the storm until 1873, when discipline within the parliamentary party began to crack. He regarded the electoral defeat of 1874 as the sharpest expression of public disapprobation of a government that he ever remembered, and retired from the leadership of the party to lick his wounds. Nevertheless the impact of Gladstone's first ministry on Victorian England, the impetus it gave to a second age of reform, cannot be denied. It saw the blossoming of that very English brand of liberal government—Gladstonian Liberalism.

2 Gladstonian Liberalism The most obvious characteristic of Gladstonian Liberalism was the attempt to establish equality of opportunity in Britain. Jobbery, nepotism and patronage of one sort or another still exist, and are, perhaps, part of the human condition. Even so the principle that birth and breeding alone rather than intellect and energy determined one's level in society was shattered by the legislation of Gladstone's two great ministries. Class privileges were slow to disappear, but by unbarring the doors of political, cultural and economic opportunity Gladstone began the process whereby the collective state replaced the hierarchial.

The Civil Service had been recruited by a system of patronage for centuries, but the increasing complexity of administration, as the state gradually extended its control over more and more aspects of communal life, demanded an ability, devotion and expertise that patronage was failing to provide. In fairness it should be remembered that the system of political nomination, whereby members of the government were able to dispense administrative posts to their relatives, friends and supporters, did produce in the nineteenth century administrators of the calibre of Chadwick and Kay-Shuttleworth. Nor was Civil Service reform new. In 1853 Macaulay's recommendation that the Indian Civil Service should be thrown open to all by means of competitive examination had been accepted, and was the first breach in the wall of privilege. This was followed by the report in 1854 of the Northcote-Trevelyan enquiry, which Gladstone as Chancellor of the Exchequer had set up to determine the lines which reform might take. Little progress, however, was made between 1854 and 1870. Even in the year the Act was passed there was strong Whig resistance within the Liberal Cabinet to the full sweep of open competition that Lowe advocated. Lowe complained that Clarendon and Granville at the Foreign and Colonial offices had 'one rule for the rich and another for the poor'.

The Act of 1871 established the principle that normal entrance to a career in the Civil Service, an exception being made of the Foreign Office through the opposition of Clarendon, was to depend on open competition. At the same time it established three grades—clerical, executive and administrative. Intellect rather than breeding was to become the passport of entry into the Civil Service. A meritocracy was to replace the influence of the aristocracy. The Fulton Report of 1968 on the Civil Service has perhaps made us more aware of the weakness of intellectual amateurism, but it is still possible to agree with Morley's conclusion: 'The Act placed the whole educated intellect of the country at the service and disposal of the state, stimulated the acquisition of knowledge, and rescued some of the most important duties in the life of the nation from the narrow class to whom they had hitherto been confined.'

The Army Regulation Bill of 1871, which Edward Cardwell, the War Secretary, introduced, had as its object the intention 'to combine in one harmonious whole all the branches of our military forces'. At the same time Cardwell combined efficiency with the career open to talents, for the Bill also abolished purchase, the practice whereby an officer not only bought his commission but also had the right to sell it for what he could get, rather like a shopkeeper selling his business. Cardwell was unable to shift the Duke of Cambridge from his position as Commander-in-Chief, despite the Duke's opposition to reform. The Queen insisted that the post belong to a member of the royal family, but an Order in Council subordinated him, the Surveyor-General of the Ordnance and the Financial Secretary to the Secretary of State for War, who was of course a minister of the Crown and a politician. Cardwell's Bill also carried out the reorganisation of the regiments, placing all infantry of the line on a territorial basis. New county areas were designated, each containing two battalions of the old regulars; these linked battalions took it in turn to serve overseas. In addition officers of the local militia were removed from the control of the Lord Lieutenant of the county and were to be appointed by the War Office. In 1869 Cardwell had also begun to withdraw troops from the self-governing colonies in order to encourage them to raise their own local forces.

The Martini-Henry rifle was introduced by Cardwell into the infantry, the first satisfactory breech-loading rifle to be supplied to the British army, but he failed to overcome the opposition of the artillery officers to new equipment, just as he failed to reorganise the cavalry regiments with their strongly entrenched officer caste. Such opposition was to wear Cardwell out by 1874, but not before he had abolished bounty money for recruits, reduced the short service minimum from twelve to six years, and abolished flogging as a punishment in peacetime. Flogging was abolished completely by the Liberals in 1881.

Cardwell's Bill of 1871 was intensely unpopular in privileged circles, especially the abolition of purchase. The purchase of commissions had first been abolished by the soldier king, William III, but Queen Anne restored it. Cardwell's Bill, though hotly contested, passed the Commons, only to be firmly rejected by the Lords. In the House of Commons Disraeli, though officially opposing the Bill as a government measure, carefully left most of the criticism to service members. The debate on the Bill in both Houses was significant in that it presented in modified form the two major constitutional issues of the next forty years. First, the colonels opposing the Bill in the Commons were accused of 'endeavouring to baffle the majority by mere consumption of time', and thus, as Ensor has pointed out, they provide the first example of obstruction in the modern sense in the very first parliament elected on a wide franchise. Secondly, the debate in the Lords presented for the first time since 1832 a clear class conflict with the Commons on a class issue. The incompatibility of Liberalism and aristocratic privilege had emerged.

Despite the opposition to the Bill the government was determined on it, not least Gladstone, who persuaded the Queen to secure the abolition of purchase by Royal Warrant—the same means by which Queen Anne had restored it. When it became apparent that the use of the Warrant did not include compensation, the Lords reopened the debate on the original Bill, and passed it without difficulty. The use of the Royal Warrant, though constitutional, was regarded as sharp practice by Gladstone's critics, both the Conservatives, who rightly felt that they had been tricked, and the radical Liberals, who mistrusted the royal prerogative on principle. To Disraeli it seemed a 'shameful and avowed conspiracy of the Cabinet', but to Gladstone it was a proper and rather obvious way to assert the will of the elected majority against the obstruction of the officer caste.

Cardwell's reforms were of great significance. The weaknesses of the British army had been exposed in the Crimean War, and were reinforced by the rise of Prussia's professional army, which distinguished itself at the battles of Sadova in 1866 and Sedan in 1870. Although the reorganisation of the army did much to destroy Gladstone's popularity with the privileged classes, the reforms were justified by the excellent performance of the army in the colonial campaigns of the next forty years. Cardwell's concern for the welfare of the ranks encouraged enlistment of a better type of soldier and enabled an adequate reserve to be built up. Cardwell was able to leave the army estimates lower than he found them and yet to increase the strength of the army in the United Kingdom by twenty-five battalions, 156 field guns, and abundant stores, whilst the reserves available for foreign service were raised by over 30,000 men. Gladstone gave Cardwell his full support, for the reforms were both humanitarian and egalitarian, and—to his marked satisfaction—they were secured without extra cost.

University reform, unlike army reform, was not new. Undergraduates at Oxford and Cambridge had been relieved of religious tests in 1854, whilst in the first half of the century the universities of London and Durham were establishing new standards of teaching and research. The University Tests Act of 1871, whereby all teaching posts at Oxford and Cambridge were no longer confined to Anglicans but were opened to men of any religious belief, carried the egalitarian reforming zeal of the Liberals into the ancient universities. The reform was not merely an attack on the privileges of the established Church, but also cleared the sectarian controversy out of the way of much-needed academic reform. This was encouraged later by Disraeli's government, which established a commission of enquiry into the finances of the colleges, and then passed an Act of Parliament making their extensive revenues more available for the purposes of education.

Gladstone and his governments did not attack the tradition of privilege merely for its vices, but because they sought to create not only a more just society, but also a more efficient one. A less controversial reform, one concerned with efficiency rather than combating privilege, was Lord Selborne's Judicature Act of 1873. The Act fused together the common law courts and the courts of equity, the latter being late medieval and Tudor additions to the legal system in an attempt to fill the gaps in the older common law system. From 1873 they were to be administered concurrently in every court, the rules of equity prevailing where there was conflict. In addition the seven courts which made up the old system were united under one Supreme Court of Judicature, which made possible a future streamlining of the system. The only serious opposition to the Act came from the the House of Lords, which objected to the abolition of its appeal jurisdiction. Disraeli came to its defence, for he saw in such action the evil influence of continental judicatures threatening the soundness of British traditions, and in 1876 Lord Cairns passed an Act restoring a final appeal to the House of Lords, where it still remains. Ensor describes Selborne's achievement as 'a piece of tidying up upon the largest scale in a field littered with the most venerable survivals from the middle ages'.

Perhaps the most far-reaching of the Liberal reforms in Gladstone's first ministry, even if it was not recognised at the time, was the 1870 Education Act. The Act left the churches in control of their own schools, and increased their grants, but where there was inadequate provision of schools, local School Boards were to be set up to build and run additional schools, though on a non-compulsory and fee-paying basis. These School Boards were to be elected by the ratepayers, and, as well as receiving a central government grant, were empowered to levy an additional local rate for their schools. They were expressly forbidden to provide denominational religious instruction. The Act seems in the 1970s a sensible and constructive one, and is rightly regarded as the foundation of the present state educational system, but in the 1870s it aroused bitter opposition in both religious and secular quarters.

It could be argued that the 1870 Education Act was the greatest achievement of Gladstone's first administration; it was certainly in many ways the most typical piece of Liberal legislation. First it had social consequences of tremendous effect, yet it was still within the sphere of self-help, with the state intervening but not taking over. Secondly it was an attack on privilege, this time on the right of the Church to control education. But rather than being revolutionary it was full of compromise. W. E. Forster, the Bradford woollen-mill owner from a Quaker family, who introduced the Bill, pointed out that the aim 'is to complete the present voluntary system, to fill up gaps . . . not to destroy the existing system in introducing a new one'. It was hoped that the Act would not only provide an efficient system of education but also a cheap one. Finally the Act, like so many other Liberal measures, was unpopular in that it offended the Nonconformists, many of whom hoped for secular education, by giving grants to Church schools, and also offended churchmen, who hoped for an extension of their control, by setting up Board schools in which religious teaching was non-denominational. Once again, despite all of the opposition, the government persisted in carrying the Act through.

Since the first grant of 1833 Parliament had been providing money for education, and in 1839 a Committee of the Privy Council for Education had been established to administer the money. Robert Lowe had introduced the first Code of Education in 1860, and in its revised form of 1862 this had marked the beginning of government legislation. Forster, in introducing his Bill, made clear the limitations of education provision before 1870. The basic problem was that the system of schools controlled by the voluntary bodies was incomplete. Forster established that on average attendance there were hardly more than one million children between six and twelve at school, whilst one and a half million were not at school at all. Furthermore, this attendance was unevenly distributed between the country areas, which were best served, and the large industrial cities where there was often a disastrous lack of proper provision, in particular Liverpool, Leeds and Birmingham. Another problem was that the quality of existing schools also varied. Forster's conclusion was that there was a growing need for the co-ordination of educational effort by the state. However, though the problems were easy to identify, and the solution of building more schools seemed obvious, the search for this solution raised problems of its own. The government was forced to compromise with the factions that sought to destroy the Bill, not least because many of these factions were Liberal party supporters.

Many manufacturers feared the withdrawal of cheap child labour if education was made compulsory, though they rationalised their fear into sympathy for parents who could not afford to send their children to school. Compulsion was, therefore, not written into the Act; School Boards were empowered to pass bye-laws to that effect only if they wished, and to pay the fees of poor children from the rates.

There was also considerable alarm about the possible cost. The Act was intended to provide schools for the labouring poor, and the costs were therefore to be kept to a minimum. To avoid a vast increase in the central government grant, deficiencies in the income of the new School Boards, after they had been paid their grant and collected their fees, were to be made up from local education rates, though these were not to exceed threepence in the pound. This decision negated the idea of a centrally controlled system of education and established a partnership between the national voluntary bodies, the state and the local community which is still a characteristic of the English system of education.

The national voluntary bodies were in the main the churches. Popular opinion was rallied behind two organisations. The National Education Union was essentially Anglican in character, was in favour of strengthening the voluntary system, in which it had the largest share of the cake, and was opposed to secularisation. The National Education League, in which Joseph Chamberlain first achieved a national reputation, wanted universal, gratuitous and compulsory secular education. Many Nonconformists, who had lost the race in the voluntary sector, supported the League. During the passage of the Bill through Parliament the issue became centred on the problem of the kind of religious education to be provided in the Board Schools. Forster's original intention was to allow the democratically elected School Boards to decide for themselves. Under pressure from the League, and on the instigation of Gladstone, the Cowper-Temple clause was added, stipulating that only non-denominational religious education was to be provided in schools receiving rate aid. Thus an unsatisfactory compromise was established, which has persisted. Both the League and the Union felt that they had been betrayed, and Gladstone found that the acrimony of the struggle in Parliamen had also spread to the country.

The Nonconformists were particularly disgruntled. They had looked upon the disestablishment of the Irish Church in 1869 as the first instalment of a popular and radical Liberal policy, but Gladstone had intended it as a step in the conciliation of Ireland. The fear that they had been deceived was crystallised by the survival of church schools. Gladstone seemed to have broken his alliance with the popular elements in the party as soon as it had been made. One result was his defeat in the 1874 election. It was not until 1876 that Gladstone's agitation against the Bulgarian atrocities reunited him with the main stream of the party.

Despite the controversy and the shortcomings of the Act, it remains a remarkable piece of social legislation, playing a vital part in civilising the masses in the nation's vast industrial cities. G. M. Young has pointed out that the Act was, 'for most English people, the first sensible impact of the administrative state on their private lives', and that 'it meant for hundreds of thousands their first glimpse of a life of cleanliness and order, light and air'.

Gladstone's main preoccupation in the 1870 session of Parliament had been with his Irish Land Bill, but his personal contribution to the passing of the Education Act was far greater than Morley suggests when he remarks that Gladstone 'rather acquiesced than led'. Gladstone worked closely with Forster in preparing the Cabinet papers for the Bill, and he supported Forster's desire for a Bill in the 1870 session, when other members of the Cabinet preferred to procrastinate in the hope of avoiding in some way inevitable torrent of opposition. It was Gladstone too who made the key appointments of moderate denominationalists during the committee stage of the Bill, and who thus helped to ensure acceptance of the Cowper-Temple clause, which he had himself suggested. Gladstone, who had been a keen advocate of the Church's role in education, later admitted; 'I have never made greater personal concessions of opinion than I did on the Education Bill.'

Disraeli found his part much easier to play. Although he accepted the extension of elementary education, he took little part in the debates on the Education Act of 1870, except to express concern over the teaching of religion by the laity in the Board Schools. In power, the Conservatives passed Sandon's Education Act in 1876, which went a step further towards compulsory education. The Act declared it was the duty of all parents to see that their children received adequate instruction, and imposed penalties on those who failed. It is clear, however, that in attempting to secure attendance through parents the intention of the Act was to prevent an extension of the power of the secular School Boards. Disraeli resisted the more obvious efforts of the churches to reassert their power during his administration, for he was not prepared to endanger his party's broad mass appeal by excursions into the controversy over educational reform. It was left to the Liberals in Mundella's Act of 1880 to compel School Boards to set up attendance committees, though Gladstone at first was opposed to the Act because it smacked of 'construction'.

The initial sign of Gladstone's abilities, and the original foundations of his own brand of Liberalism, had first emerged with his support of free trade when he was Chancellor of the Exchequer. In 1868 the country expected financial wonders from Gladstone's government. It was to be disappointed. With the triumph of free trade, the permanence of income tax, and the absence of all but colonial wars, fiscal policy was generally unadventurous in the Indian summer of Victorian prosperity. Until 1871 Robert Lowe as Chancellor of the Exchequer had a healthy revenue and thrifty colleagues. However, in order to raise money for the increased army expenditure inspired by the Franco-Prussian War, Lowe proposed to raise a million pounds by a tax on matches. Match manufacturers protested that it would ruin their trade, and unfortunately for Lowe the principal match factory was in London. A protest outside the House of Commons, largely by 'match girls' dressed in their rags, won much sympathy, and Lowe was forced to withdraw his tax and raise the money by increasing the income tax. Disraeli disdainfully dismissed the whole manoeuvre as 'harum-scarum'. Generally the rest of the government's term of office was plain sailing in fiscal matters. Gladstone became his own Chancellor of the Exchequer in 1873, and was even confident enough to promise the abolition of the income tax as part of his unsuccessful bid to win the election of 1874. Sir Stafford Northcote, Disraeli's Chancellor of the Exchequer, was content to lower income tax by a penny and to spend the rest on increasing the army estimates and abolishing sugar duties.

The only real departure in monetary policy in these years was in fact made by the Conservatives with the establishment of a new Sinking Fund in 1875. The idea had first been employed by Walpole in the eighteenth century, and Northcote revived it. The plan was simply to pay off a part of the National Debt each year by putting aside in the Fund slightly more than was needed to pay the yearly interest. This would provide ever-increasing margins over the years as the lessening of the debt reduced the sum due in interest. A gap in Gladstone's fiscal policy was thus filled, but the danger, as Walpole had discovered, was the temptation to raise the Fund to meet emergencies. By 1879 Northcote, indeed, found himself raiding the Fund to help pay for the Zulu War.

The depression which had begun in agriculture and was spreading, together with expensive colonial ventures, led to a gradually increasing income tax, and the intention to abolish the tax became submerged. This was no less true in the period after 1880, when until 1882 Gladstone once again took upon himself the double task of Prime Minister and Chancellor of the Exchequer. Gladstone enjoyed the detail of fiscal work, but such indulgences when he was Prime Minister clearly left him less time for the general functions of leadership.

The great chances in financial policy had come before 1868. The liberation of commerce, which had helped stimulate industrial development, helped to create also those radically-minded industrial classes which sought their own progressive fulfilment, politically as well as economically, through the destruction of the traditional caste society of Britain. Gladstone as Chancellor of the Exchequer before 1868 had contributed to the economic resurgence, and as Prime Minister he prepared the way for political emergence. A post in the Civil Service, a commission in the army, a college fellowship, had all been considered species of property until 1868. When to his interference with these are added Gladstone's disestablishment of the Irish Church, his introduction of two Irish Land Acts, his support for a separate parliament in Dublin, for School Boards independent of the Church, and for a further extension of the franchise, it is not surprising that to the propertied classes in general he was an ogre undermining the fundamental principles of society. His defence in 1880 of the atheistic Charles Bradlaugh's right to sit in the House of Commons again offended churchmen. The passing of the Married Women's Property Act in 1882, which granted to married women the same rights over their property as single women, increased the alarm of the propertied classes. It was this concerted attack on prejudice and privilege which was the essence of Gladstonian Liberalism.

3 Social reform   Social reform in the 1870s, in the sense of the reforms intended to improve directly the condition of the labouring classes, is inevitably associated with Disraeli and the the Conservatives rather than with the Liberals. This was Disraeli's intention, and there can be no doubt that he succeeded. The problem for the historian is to estimate how much of Disraeli's achievement in this sphere is myth and how much reality. Does he deserve the titles 'social reformer' and 'Tory democrat'?

If Gladstone and the Liberals launched a new era of reform by the spontaneous combustion of their mixture of talents, then it could be said that Disraeli made sure the Conservatives had their part to play by his more cautious approach to power and office. Like Gladstone in 1868, Disraeli found it necessary in forming his second ministry in 1874 to compromise with the traditional leaders of the party, and he paid due regard to the predominance of the landed interest. Both Carnarvon and Salisbury, who had resigned over the 1867 Reform Act, were found places in the Cabinet. Salisbury was not entirely happy, but he could find no political issue on which to refuse office. However Disraeli, unlike Gladstone, preferred to sidestep challenges to his position and policies rather than meet them head on. The barrenness of Disraeli's domestic legislation after 1876, and the distant interest he himself took in matters of social reform, may not have been due to inertia and declining health, as his apologists claim, but perhaps to an unwillingness to risk his personal position and party unity by antagonising his less enthusiastic adherents in the Conservative party. The government's increasing interest in foreign affairs not only satisfied Disraeli's vanity, but also drew the interests of the nation away from domestic matters that could prove controversial. Thus there were tactical reasons why social reforms did not play an even bigger part in Conservative policies.

Disraeli did not declare his motto '*Sanitas sanitatum, omnia sanitas*' until 1872, but one of his last acts as Prime Minister in 1868 had been to appoint a Royal Sanitary Commission. The Commission reported in 1871, and it was the Liberals who were the first to act upon it. The Commission recommended 'that the present fragmentary and confused Sanitary Legislation should be consolidated, and that the administration of Sanitary Law should be made uniform, universal and imperative throughout the kingdom'. The Local Government Act of 1871 reorganised the central machinery for health administration under a Minister as the Local Government Board. A further piece of Liberal legislation in 1872 established the Urban and Rural Sanitary Authorities, which were to be responsible in their local areas for public health, and were required to appoint Inspectors of Nuisances and a Medical Officer. The Liberals thus provided an improved administrative framework on which the Conservatives could build, and claim all the credit.

The Conservative Public Health Act of 1875 established a system of powers, compulsion and checks ranging from responsibility for sewage and drainage to providing public lavatories and controlling cellar-dwellings. It was largely a codification of previous legislation, and confirmed that the administration of public health was to be in the hands of the new authorities established by the Liberals. To the 1875 Act the Conservatives added in the same year the Sale of Food and Drugs Act, which remained the most important piece of legislation on adulteration until 1928. The Artisans' Dwellings Act, also of 1875, empowered local authorities for the first time to pull down slums and substitute healthier buildings. The Act, however, was only permissive, and Richard Cross the Home Secretary who introduced it pointed out 'that it is not the duty of the Government to provide any class of citizens with any of the necessaries of life . . . it would inevitably tend to make that class depend, not on themselves, but upon what was done for them elsewhere'. Gladstone would undoubtedly have agreed with him. The result was that six years later only ten of the eighty-seven English and Welsh towns to which it applied had made any attempt to implement its provisions. An Act of 1876 again attacked for the first time the pollution of rivers by industrial waste, by no means a late-twentieth-century phenomenon. It forbade the dumping of solids in rivers, and allowed the dumping of liquids only if they were non-poisonous.

Cross at the Home Office was largely responsible for the drafting of these Conservative measures. His Enclosure of Commons Act in 1876 provided an additional bonus to the general welfare of the people by restricting the rights of landowners to absorb public land into their estates. This was followed by the Epping Forest Act in 1878 which saved that area for the enjoyment of all. As Cross himself said, summarizing the government's achievements in public health, 'What the people of this country want almost as much as they want food, is the air which they breathe and the health which they enjoy.' The legislation of these years laid the foundations of modern public health so thoroughly and lastingly that no major changes were required for over sixty years.

Like the problems of public health before 1870, the position of the trade unions since the repeal of the Combination Laws remained vague and confused, though the confusion sprang from judicial decisions rather than unco-ordinated legislation. The main issues for the unions were the right to strike and their right to hold corporate property and enforce agreements by suing in the law courts. The Trade Union Act of 1871, introduced by Gladstone's Home Secretary Bruce, provided that a trade union should not be considered an illegal body merely because it was in restraint of trade; the right to strike was recognised. The Act also allowed a union to register under the Friendly Society Acts, provided its rules were not criminal; the unions were recognised as corporate bodies and their funds given the protection of the law. The limitations of the Liberal parliamentary mind were, however, revealed by the Criminal Law Amendment Act of 1871, which forbade picketing of any kind, and thus rendered impotent the right to strike. Trade unions could strike, but they could not make their strike effective against blacklegging.

These two Acts, so contrary to each other, reveal Gladstone's ignorance of working-class conditions. The ban on picketing was clearly an error of judgement, though Gladstone believed that decisions should be freely arrived at by both employers and employees. Coercion of an individual's opinions, even for the good of the group, was repugnant to him. The chief object of the trade unions came to be the repeal of the obnoxious Act, and Disraeli took the opportunity to woo them to the Conservative party. Nevertheless, at a time when official opinion was still strongly opposed to trade unionism it was Gladstone's government which first brought to the attention of Parliament a national problem which had long been neglected.

Cross's Conspiracy and Protection of Property Act in 1875 repealed the Criminal Law Amendment Act of 1871, expressly permitting peaceful picketing, and going on to permit trade unions to do as a group whatever was lawful for an individual, without fear of being charged with conspiracy. Cross also introduced the Employers and Workmen Act, which put master and man on an equal footing regarding breaches of contract. Previously a breach of contract by a workman was classified as a criminal offence, but that of an employer merely a civil one. Now both were to be regarded as civil offences subject to damages rather than imprisonment. At last the trade unions had become a recognised element of the capitalist society which, in the eyes of many unionists, had at one time sought to enslave them.

Disraeli had taken a keen interest in this legislation and had supported Cross successfully against the more faint-hearted members of the Cabinet. He told Lady Chesterfield that the legislation 'will gain and retain for the Conservatives the lasting affection of the working classes'. Such affection was also encouraged by the Factory Act of 1874, which at last accomplished the ten-hour day. The work of Shaftesbury in this field was completed, just as in 1875 he himself was able to pass a Bill which forbade sweeps to carry on their trade without an annual licence from the police. The police were to enforce the laws regulating the use of chimney-sweep boys, as Shaftesbury had long urged. A further Factory Act in 1878 codified and rationalised the factory legislation passed since 1833, and abolished the arbitrary distinction between factories and workshops as places where more or fewer than fifty persons were employed. A more sensible distinction was made between the use and non-use of mechanical power.

Such definite achievements for the working classes prompted Alexander MacDonald of the Amalgamated Society of Engineers to declare; 'The Conservative Party has done more for the working class in five years than the Liberals have done in fifty.' On such remarks is the myth of Tory democracy founded. It contrasts sharply with the words of the popular Rochdale poet Edwin Waugh:

> Let England remember the days of old,
>> When the Liberal leaders ruled her,
> Ere she squandered in bloodshed her hard-won gold
>> And a Beaconsfield be-fooled her:
> When peace and plenty went hand in hand,
>> And her toilers lived in clover,
> And the aim of those who ruled the land
>> Was justice the wide world over.

Disraeli was clearly seeking to win friends and gain votes in the urban areas, and his strategy undoubtedly helped to create the Tory working man. In the counties his tactics were different. The landed interest's support for the Conservative party was generally taken for granted, and this was greatly strengthened by Gladstone's Irish Land Act of 1870, for an attack on Irish property alarmed all property owners. It was clear, however, that if the landlords suffered, the tenants benefited. Disraeli's limited opposition to the Bill was mainly concerned with support for the clear principle of freedom of contract. By pursuing this strategy he was successful in preventing a split between tenant and landlord. This, like Gladstone's other attacks on property rights, encouraged further the shift from Liberal to Conservative amongst the Whigs in the House of Lords. It may seem all the more confounding then that the Conservatives lost ground in the rural areas after 1880.

The reasons for this decline in support are not in fact too hard to find. The stability of the mid-Victorian period had partly rested on the balance of prosperity between industry and agriculture, but that balance was destroyed by the depression of the 1870s to the detriment of agriculture. Here the Conservative social conscience surprisingly reached its limit. The fiscal policies of the Conservatives gave only slight assistance by removing duties on horses, and the hated malt tax was not abolished. In 1875 the Agricultural Holdings Act, which, by offering compensation for improvements, extended the Irish Land Act to English tenants, was introduced personally by Disraeli. The tenant farmers disliked it, however, because it was permissive rather than compulsory, whilst landlords were offended because they did not like any interference with their property rights. The government were unwilling to do anything more to relieve distress. They ignored the growing demand for reciprocity or protection, and though a Royal Commission under the Duke of Richmond was set up to examine the problem, no action was taken. Disraeli had converted the party to free trade and he held the ship firmly on course. Taxes on food would be electorally damaging in the towns. Unfortunately for the Conservatives the militant Farmers' Alliance supported the Liberals. The government's policy undermined aristocratic control of the county constituencies, as the results of the 1880 and 1885 elections indicate. In previous years the Conservatives had been able to blame the government of the day for unpopular agricultural policies, but in 1879, when bad harvests produced the peak of the depression, they were themselves the government.

After the 1880 election it was the Liberals who came to the assistance of the tenants and small farmers. The Ground Game Act of 1880 gave the occupier an inalienable right to destroy hares and rabbits on the land he rented. In 1880 also the malt tax, a long-standing grievance of farmers, was converted to a beer duty. The Settled Land Act of 1882 gave tenants of an estate for life the right to grant further leases. In 1884 the farm labourer was enfranchised. Although in the 1885 election the Liberals did not do as well in the boroughs as they expected, they were saved by the votes cast for them in the county constituencies.

The Merchant Shipping Act of 1876, which established the famous Plimsoll line, and which received considerable attention at the time because of Samuel Plimsoll's extravagant behaviour, and the hint that the shipowners where attempting to block the measure, also illustrates the folly of overstating the Conservative party's claim to be the party of social reform. The load line was introduced through Plimsoll's pressuring, but it could be drawn where the shipowner thought fit until the Board of Trade intervened in 1890. Before 1890 the Liberals, inspired by Chamberlain, had secured further restrictions by a Grain Cargoes Act, and had secured better wages for seamen with another Act. A social conscience was a condition of the time, not the perquisite of a party.

The Education Act of 1870 arose out of Liberal concern for working-class literacy, and the Liberal social conscience also included a dislike of the evil of drunkenness. When in 1872 Bruce as Home Secretary managed, at the second attempt, to pass his Licensing Act, the Liberals realised from the force of the opposition that they would pay dearly for their consciences. The Act provided for the closing down of public houses in those areas where they were too many, imposed limitations on opening hours and introduced regulations against adulteration. The passage of the Bill led to rioting in various towns, nearly every public house in the United Kingdom became an active committee room of the Conservative party, and even the Bishop of Peterborough joined in, declaring that he would like to see 'England free better than England sober'. Gladstone always believed the Act was the root cause of defeat in 1874, and Ensor dates the government's unpopularity from 1871, the year in which Bruce first attempted to pass the Bill. Ensor also claims that the defection of the brewers and distillers from the Liberal party—for like other industrialists they had tended to be Liberal—helps to explain why the Conservatives were more popular in the forty years after 1871 than the forty years before. This cannot be verified, however, for party funds were then secret, and precise evidence is not available. Such an interpretation is now suspect. The Conservatives did, however, carry a Licensing Act in 1874 which made prompt concessions to the liquor interests, though, in respect of closing public houses and modifying opening hours, it did not repeal as much of Bruce's legislation as the liquor interests wanted.

Conservative claims to be the party of social reform in the nineteenth century obviously should not be accepted wholesale. The flow of Conservative reform was to stop after 1876 with Disraeli's declining health, Irish obstruction and the more pressing problems of overseas affairs. The same fate befell Gladstone after 1880, and if it had not been for Chamberlain's badgering there would have been little reform of any kind in Gladstone's second ministry. Both Gladstone and Disraeli were also suspicious of compulsion and direct state interference. Neither took any great interest in the details of the work on social reform, with the exception of Disraeli's interest in his government's trade union legislation. It has been claimed that social reform was a policy with which Disraeli sought to win the new voters to the Conservative cause, but it is strange that he said nothing about it in his election manifesto of 1880. Even Cross, the main agent of social reform, in his own election address scarcely mentioned the subject.

Although Disraeli's second ministry secured the biggest instalment of social reform by any government in the nineteenth century, it would be inaccurate to conclude that it was the Conservatives who made the change from laissez-faire to state intervention. The Conservatives no less than the Gladstonian Liberals were opposed to collectivism, and most of their reforms were permissive rather than compulsory—a factor which reduced their effectiveness. With regard to Disraeli's social reforms Blake points out; 'It is an exaggeration to regard them as the product of a fundamentally different political philosophy from that of the Liberals, or to see in them the fulfilment of some concept of paternalistic Tory democracy which had been adumbrated by Disraeli in opposition to Peel during the 1840s and now at last reached fruition.'

There would, therefore, appear to have been a strong element of mere vote-catching in Disraeli's advocacy of social reform and the other aspects of Tory democracy. Social reform for Disraeli was a means to an end, not an end in itself. His great success was to put an end to the Conservatism which preached loyalty to ancient institutions, but which did not govern. Disraeli thus emerges as Peel's real heir. Disraeli disagreed with Peel's method rather than his objective. Through 'Tory democracy' Disraeli hoped that these ancient institutions would not be discarded but would be revitalised by 'the invigorating energies of an educated and enfranchised people'. Disraeli explained precisely what these institutions were: 'I mean the splendour of the Crown, the lustre of the Peerage, the privileges of the Commons, the rights of the poor. I mean that harmonious union, that magnificent concord of all interests, of all classes, on which our national greatness depends.' Despite his failure in the 1880 election the later prestige of the Conservative party indicates that Disraeli was successful in his attempt to interpret original Tory principles within the setting of the modern world.

4 Further parliamentary reform If Disraeli believed that the masses preferred social to parliamentary reform this would help to explain why after 1867 he left the problems of parliamentary reform for the Liberals to solve. The Liberals certainly claimed all the credit for the enfranchisement of the people in the nineteenth century. It may well be, however, that Disraeli avoided further adventures with parliamentary reform because the furore he created within his own party in 1867 had warned him off risking further trouble. Disraeli was also perhaps concerned that reform which would come after 1867, when borough democracy had been conceded, would be bound to affect vested interests in the counties, which it was assumed were largely Conservative. Liberal credit for the 1867 Reform Act has been hotly contested. The Liberals' part in later reforms also needs examination.

The demand for a secret ballot had figured in advanced programmes of reform for well over a century. The final impetus to the ballot came from the revelation of scandalous practices in the 1868 election, when 111 petitions were presented alleging malpractices. The Ballot Act of 1872 ended the brawling and corruption of the hustings. Opposition to secrecy came mainly from landlords and employers, for voters, it was feared, would be able to act independently. This opposition was largely, but not entirely, Conservative, though Disraeli took little part in the debate, for the ballot was also supported by many Conservatives in the urban areas, where they were anxious to win votes. Gladstone was in favour, but Hartington, then the Liberal Postmaster-General and leader of the Whigs, accepted the measure of 1872 with the utmost reluctance, hoping that it might be only temporary, and that one day voting might be free, tranquil and open as well.

Despite the hopes and fears raised in debate in 1872, the Act did not win popular approval for the Liberals, nor did it have profound effects upon England. There were still opportunities for the corrupt politician to buy votes. The Liberals, however, continued to clear up electoral corruption and to give the Act of 1872 effective force. This was largely accomplished by Sir Henry James, the Attorney-General, who introduced his Corrupt Practices Act in 1883. This clearly defined the precise amount of money that could be spent on each electoral campaign, and made illegal every form of bribery and undue influence. Thus the business of conducting an election in the future was to be the task of members of the party working for their principles, rather than that of hirelings working for money. The Act was overshadowed, however, by the great achievement in parliamentary reform of Gladstone's second ministry, the Franchise of 1884.

The Act of 1884 created a uniform householder and lodger franchise for the whole of the United Kingdom, based on the franchise created for the English boroughs in 1867. In addition it provided for an occupational franchise for those with lands or tenements worth £10 a year. The electorate was increased by something just over two million voters. An accompanying Redistribution Act in 1885 resulted in seventy-nine towns of fewer than 15,000 inhabitants ceasing to be separate constituencies.

Thirty-six towns of fewer than 50,000 inhabitants lost one of their two members. The universities and the medium-sized boroughs retained two members, but the rest of the country was divided into single-member constituencies. By dividing the large towns into electoral wards purely working-class constituencies were created for the first time. Also for the first time the Act included Ireland on the same terms as the rest of the country. Not surprisingly this major instalment of parliamentary reform did not have an easy birth.

The initiative for the Act came from the Radicals in the Liberal party, who believed their efforts had returned Gladstone to power in 1880, and felt that they had received little by way of legislative reward. Their leader Joseph Chamberlain had been relegated to an inferior position in the Cabinet as President of the Board of Trade. But Chamberlain could not be silenced, and by the end of 1883 he had managed to shame the Cabinet into finding the time and the courage to introduce a Bill which would finally clear the last anomaly of the franchise—the distinction between the democratic towns and the aristocratic countryside. Hartington, now at the War Office, agreed to the reform in principle and managed under Gladstone's persuasion to swallow the unpalatable details of the Bill.

The Bill passed the Commons easily, but the Conservatives in the Lords, led by Salisbury, the leader of the party and a proven opponent of reform, were very hostile. Rather than risk a head-on conflict, the Lords proposed that a Redistribution Bill should be passed first. The Conservatives were hoping that either local jealousies over redistribution would kill both Bills or, as Disraeli had once argued, it would appear they were taking the initiative through the Lords, and therefore deserved the credit for reform. The reaction of the radical Liberals led by Chamberlain and John Morley (later Gladstone's biographer) was to ignore the Lords' demands and stir up the passions of the country with the cry 'The Peers against the People'. Gladstone, however, intervened, and by direct negotiation with Salisbury secured the passage of both Bills. As in 1832 and 1867 parliamentary reform once again emerged as a compromise between the parties.

Gladstone hoped that his franchise reform would bring out the highest qualities in the new electorate and that 'the sense of justice, which abides tenaciously in the masses will never knowingly join hands with the fiend of Jingoism'. Under the impact of the secret ballot, the Corrupt Practices Act and, most important of all, the increase in the electorate, effective electoral corruption ended as the nomination borough or county passed away. The initiative, if not all the details of parliamentary reform, had been a Liberal one. Gladstone had played a leading rôle once again in the passing of the 1884 and 1885 Acts; together they were perhaps the last, but by no means the least achievement of Gladstonian Liberalism.

5 The fickleness of the electorate Despite the ability of Gladstone and Disraeli as politicians, despite their brilliant and highly successful reforms, each man at a climax in his career was faced with a shattering electoral defeat. The 'People's William' of 1868 was disillusioned enough to retire from the leadership of the Liberal party after the electoral fiasco of 1874. The man who succeeded him with a large majority, the man who returned triumphant from the Congress of Berlin in 1878 bringing peace with honour, was equally demoralised by the Conservative defeat in the election of 1880. All reforming governments acquire enemies by the very nature of their task, but the caprice of the electorate in 1874 and 1880 demands a more thorough explanation.

Why did Gladstone's great ministry, with such excellent reforming achievements to its credit, fail to win re-election in 1874? In the first place the vested interests which Gladstone had antagonised were quite formidable. Gentry families disapproved of the abolition of the purchase of commissions and the general effect of Cardwell's army reforms. There was similar resistance to open competition in the Civil Service. Even within the Liberal party there was some alarm amongst the Whigs, not least at the Ballot Act, which decreased the landlords' influence at elections. The House of Lords accepted the tinkering with 'property' involved in the Irish Land Act, but they and their fellow landlords were not happy with it. Many clergy did not approve of the disestablishment of the Irish Church nor the University Tests Act, both of which undermined the supremacy of the Church of England in law. Disraeli, like Peel in the 1830s, became the rallying-point of those opposed to radical reform, but favouring cautious reform.

What was probably more important in the defeat of the Liberals was that their unpopularity was not confined to respectable county families. The Conservatives made gains in by-elections after 1870 not only in county divisions like Surrey or market towns like Shaftesbury, but also in the urbanised West Riding, in Hull and in Oldham. Why was this? Gladstone's foreign policy, with such measures as the submission to arbitration of American claims in the 'Alabama' dispute, affronted the Palmerstonian instinct which permeated all classes. More particularly there had been little constructive social reform to win the votes of the masses, whilst the government's attitude to trade unions, reeking as it did of laissez-faire doctrines, antagonised many. Lowe's attempt to tax matches was a propaganda gift to the opposition. Bruce's Licensing Act may have pleased the temperance movement, but it displeased the brewing interest and their customers. Gladstone's own verdict on the defeat of 1874 was; 'We have been borne down in a torrent of gin and beer'.

In addition to these troubles, the unity of the Liberal party was being undermined. It was, perhaps, the passing of the 1870 Education Act that had the most disastrous effect on the party. Bright remarked that the Bill 'was one the Tories might have proposed, but could not have passed. A Liberal government only could pass a measure so far wide of the Liberal line of march.' The Nonconformists, aided by the National Education League, were shattered by Forster's proposals, and their faith in the party was considerably shaken. They did not vote Conservative in 1874, but many seem to have abstained.

Late in 1873 Gladstone wrote to Morley: 'Divisions in the Liberal party are to be seriously apprehended from a factious spirit on questions of economy, on questions of education in relation to religion, on further parliamentary change, on the land laws.' That 'factious spirit' had already led to defeat of the

77

government by three votes over the Irish University Bill in March 1873. Gladstone had wanted to resign, but Disraeli refused office, preferring to watch the breach in the Liberal party widen. It was a sound tactic, for all discipline seemed to vanish from the Liberal ranks. Moreover a scandal in the Post Office discredited three ministers, and Gladstone became his own Chancellor of the Exchequer at a time when he should have been concentrating on the leadership. Gladstone was to offer the electorate the prospect of the abolition of income tax, though opposed in this by his service ministers, but it was not enough to win back the confidence of those he had offended. Disraeli turned on the government, comparing them to a marine landscape in South America: 'You behold a range of exhausted volcanoes. Not a flame flickers on a single pallid crest. But the situation is still dangerous. There are occasional earthquakes, and ever and anon the dark rumbling of the sea.'

The failure of the Liberals in 1873-4 was not, however, entirely due to the unpopularity of their policies and divisions within the party, for Disraeli had rallied the Conservative party to the battle. By 1874 they were a united body, ready and eager for office. How did Disraeli contribute to this victory, which the Conservatives had striven for since 1846? The question is all the more pertinent since Disraeli's position as leader of the party in 1868 was weak; indeed he was not clear of challenges to his authority until he took office in 1874.

The root cause of Disraeli's unpopularity in his party was the 1867 Reform Act. It was detested outright by many, and its failure to produce an immediate dividend in the 1868 election further condemned Disraeli's policy of supporting such a Bill, whilst the implications of borough democracy introduced new tensions into the party. E. J. Feuchtwanger in his study of Disraeli and the Tory party has indicated the general suspiciousness concerning Disraeli: 'To many Tories a Jewish literary man at the head of the party was only tolerable if he achieved results, and in electoral terms Disraeli's success had not been spectacular.' In 1869 and 1870 there were attempts to make Cranborne, the future Lord Salisbury, leader in the House of Lords, which was clearly a threat to Disraeli. Cranborne had reluctantly accepted the implications of the Reform Act, but had not yet accepted Disraeli. The latter's prime task in opposition was, therefore, to ensure his own survival. This was achieved in two ways. First he sought to take advantage of Gladstone's growing unpopularity, and secondly he successfully outlined a Conservative programme that would win votes. Disraeli's plan was not simply to raise popular enthusiasm for the party, but also to strengthen his own position amongst its traditional supporters.

Disraeli's speech in the Free Trade Hall, Manchester in April 1872 marks the end of his defensive period as leader of the party and the beginning of his more positive struggle for survival and success. In his speeches of 1872 and 1873 he emphasised his support for the monarchy and the established Church in a re-statement of traditional Toryism, and such a re-statement took up the greater part of his speeches. But Disraeli did have more to say. His support for the Empire seemed a new and unconventional policy. From the viewpoint of the twentieth century, however, it seems more obvious that Disraeli had simply put on the cloak discarded by Palmerston. It is Gladstone's seeming weakness in foreign affairs which appears as the new departure. Disraeli's real innovation was the platform of social reform as official Conservative party policy. He sketched only the outlines of such a policy without the inconvenience of details, but this was still Disraeli's personal contribution to making the Conservative party a bond between the different social classes of the nation. Gladstone might offer participation in government to the masses, but Disraeli more practically offered amelioration of their living conditions. Thus the policy which Disraeli offered was a mixture of his personal political views, which he had always held, tempered by reality and the traditional views common to all Conservatives. Innovation could be only, and he himself intended it to be only, a part of his programme.

The election of 1874 was a triumph for Disraeli and his interpretation of Conservatism, yet within six years he had to face the bitterness of electoral defeat. Why? Was it merely a combination of Disraeli's declining health, bad luck, and in particular

Gladstone's deceitful moral attack on imperialism, as Buckle (and the Queen) believed? Perhaps Disraeli, already elevated to the House of Lords as Earl of Beaconsfield, should take some of the blame.

Gladstone abandoned his first retirement in order to launch his attack on the inhumanity of Disraeli's Eastern policy and the extravagance of his ambitions for the Empire. Such was the basis of Gladstone's two Midlothian campaigns, his 'pilgrimage of passion'. At the height of his triumphs at the Congress of Berlin in 1878 Disraeli had gained a position stronger than the majority of Prime Ministers ever achieved, and it was widely held at the time, though since disputed by Hanham, that if he had gone to the country on his return from Berlin he would have been returned. But he did not, and the 'massacres' of Isandhlwana and Kabul intervened. Gladstone made full use of his opportunity with the electors in 1880. He declared that the Conservative government had 'weakened the Empire by needless wars . . . dishonoured it in the eyes of Europe by filching the island of Cyprus from the Porte . . . aggrandised Russia, lured Turkey to her dismemberment if not her ruin, replaced the Christian population of Macedonia under a degrading yoke, and loaded India with the cost and dangers of an unjustifiable war'. Disraeli could dismiss Gladstone's Midlothian campaign as 'rhodomontade and rigmarole', but the absence of any reply may well have led the public to conclude that no effective reply was possible.

The election was largely fought on matters of foreign and imperial policy, for it was this that had reunited Gladstone to the radical Nonconformists. Gladstone's address in 1877 to the National Liberal Federation, which Chamberlain had fashioned out of the Education League, at once signified the new unity of the party and Gladstone's leadership of it. Nonetheless the decline of Disraeli's energies and the increasing lack of domestic legislation after 1876, which cannot all be explained away by the increasing obstruction in the Commons by Parnell and the Irish Party, undoubtedly played their part. Furthermore H. J. Hanham in his *Elections and Party Management* has stressed the effects of the depression in undermining the Conservative government, which resisted demands for aid. For the first time militant farmers through the Farmers' Alliance supported the Liberals, and with unemployment at eleven per cent the working classes forgot the material concessions made to them before 1876. Gladstone was quick to point out also the failures in domestic matters: 'At home the ministers have neglected legislation, aggravated the public distress by continual shocks to confidence, which is the life of enterprise, augmented the public expenditure and taxation for purposes not merely unnecessary but mischievous, and plunged the finances, which were handed over to them in a state of singular prosperity, into a series of deficits unexampled in modern times.' Disraeli's failure to follow Gladstone's example and 'stump the country' is an indication not only of his ill-health, but also shows that he was less aware than Gladstone of the need to woo the new electorate he had helped to create.

Gladstone saw in the Liberal majority of forty-six over Conservatives and Irish Nationalists in the election of 1880 'the great hand of God, so evidently displayed'. He declared, 'The downfall of Beaconsfieldism is like the vanishing of some vast magnificent castle in an Italian romance.' Gladstone was elated with what was very much a personal success, but the Queen was not. She invited both Lord Hartington and Lord Granville to form a ministry, but both refused, and only then did she reluctantly summon the eager Gladstone. This was both inevitable and significant, for, as Ensor has pointed out, 'Gladstone had gone behind parliament to the people, which for the first time virtually chose its own premier'.

The election of 1880 provided Gladstone with his opportunity to undo as quickly as possible the moral harm of 'Beaconsfieldism'. Unfortunately in foreign affairs he found himself attempting to defend the status quo of the Conservatives. Irish problems, both in Ireland and in the person of Parnell at Westminister, dominated Parliament. By taking on the Chancellorship of the Exchequer Gladstone once again became bogged down in the petty details of government expenditure. In addition the issues of radical reform, the Bradlaugh controversy and Ireland produced factions once again within the Liberal party. It is not surprising that such difficulties put an almost complete stop to controversial domestic legislation. Once again the Liberal government began to disintegrate, and the news from Khartoum completed this process. A combination of Parnell and Lord Randolph Churchill, the new radical star of the Conservative party, secured an amendment to the 1885 budget on the increase of duty on beer but not on wine, and Gladstone resigned. Lord Salisbury and the Conservatives held the fort until the new electoral roll was ready, and then they too resigned.

The election of 1885 gave the Liberals a majority over the Conservatives of eighty-six, largely due to Chamberlain's 'unauthorised programme'. In his campaign Chamberlain announced his plans for reforms in education, rural conditions and local government, none of which was official party policy. In particular he advocated peasant proprietorship in England and, taken together with Liberal aid to the tenant farmers after 1880, this secured votes for the Liberals in the counties. However, the Irish had gained eighty-six seats, and with these at his disposal Parnell was presented with his opportunity. Gladstone was at last prepared to bring forward a Home Rule Bill, but this brought only divisions within his own party, defeat in the House of Commons, and the electoral disaster in the 1886 election. Something had gone wrong.

This raises the question of the part Gladstone played in the decline of the Liberal party. The usual explanation for that decline begins with Gladstone's Home Rule policy, examines the impact of the rise of the Labour party and goes on to cite the quarrel between Lloyd George and Asquith in 1918. The general election of 1880 certainly seemed to promise the Liberals a prolonged lease of power, and though the party was divided between the Whigs under Hartington and the Radicals under Chamberlain, Gladstone seemed capable of holding the ring. The latter's decision to support Home Rule in 1886, however, drove both Hartington and Chamberlain into opposition, and thus caused the defeat of 1886. Though Gladstone was still able to rally the country to the cause in the 1892 election, he was too old and his colleagues too fearful to fight the challenge of the

House of Lords over Ireland. Gladstone's retirement in 1894 and the party's defeat in the 1895 election marked the end of the first phase of Liberal decline. However, recent research into what was actually happening in the constituencies during the elections is beginning to indicate that factors were at work other than the internecine strife within the Liberal party.

The importance of the break-up of the Liberal party over Home Rule, and its results in the 1886 election, cannot be denied, but the total impact of Home Rule as a disintegrating factor can be questioned. Whigs had after all been taking part in a general exodus from the Liberal party since 1865, whilst the departure of Chamberlain still left most of the rank and file of the party with Gladstone. G. Kitson Clark, in his *An Expanding Society*, suggests that something else was causing the decline of the Liberal party. Beginning with the election of 1868 and certainly in that of 1885, when the Liberals lost in the towns and gained in the counties, he tentatively favours a theory involving a change in political allegiance in the new suburbs: 'There was a constant flow of rather wealthy people from the Whigs and Liberals to the Conservatives and the creation in the suburban areas of what were in effect single-class communities made admirably safe Tory seats.' As the rise of a Labour party helps to explain the loss of working-class votes by the Liberal party, so such a theory helps to explain the desertion of the respectable middle classes from the party, and the twenty years of almost uninterrupted Conservative rule at the end of the century.

One of the most important tasks of a party leader is to maintain party unity, to prevent the polarisation of party views by some sort of compromise. Both Gladstone and Disraeli had to face this problem in an extreme form, because the electorate to which their parties addressed themselves was going through a period of rapid extension and democratisation, which required the constant adjustment of policy to maintain an acceptable compromise. Disraeli, perhaps, was more prepared to sacrifice principle in order to secure party unity. Yet party unity was perhaps Disraeli's greatest achievement, for it provided the Conservative party with a sound basis which enabled it to survive into the twentieth century. In comparison Gladstone's more principled leadership of the Liberal party, which he involved in the toils of the Irish problem, brought disunity and electoral disaster, and greatly weakened the party's ability to survive. Ironically it was to be the renegade Joseph Chamberlain who restored some semblance of unity to the Liberal party when it realigned itself to oppose his policy of protection.

Chapter IV

Overseas policies 1868-86

1 Principles The basis of British foreign policy in the nineteenth century was the preservation of some sort of status quo—
a policy of no change. The settlement of 1815 had secured a
balance in Europe and the world which treated Britain favourably.
This favourable balance British foreign secretaries and their
leaders, including Gladstone and Disraeli, sought to defend in two
ways. First they held to a policy of non-intervention in the petty
squabbles of Europe when this was possible, for intervention might
encourage others and bring about changes that could affect
Britain's position. The second tactic, somewhat contradictory,
was to intervene in those incidents which seriously involved
British interests to ensure that any territorial change maintained
Britain's predominant interests. It was the decisions over which
issues necessitated British intervention and how such intervention should be achieved, rather than differences of principle, that
provided the grounds for conflict and disagreement between the
statesmen responsible for directing British diplomacy. How then
did differences of opinion on British policy arise between
Gladstone and Disraeli?

What is at first striking about the external policies of Gladstone
and Disraeli is the marked similarity of their aims. Greater
differences existed in their methods, but the policies of both men
were dictated by the fact that increasingly after 1870 Britain
was on the defensive. Britain had consolidated her predominant

position in the world, but the greatest danger to that position was war in Europe, where there was much activity by both great and small powers to escape from the strait-jacket imposed in 1815. Realising reluctantly the need for change, British policy attempted to secure it without war, through international agreement rather than unilateral aggrandisement.

Before 1868 Gladstone and Disraeli had often found themselves in entire agreement on foreign affairs. This was easier when they were both in opposition to Palmerston.[1] Thus in 1851 both bitterly attacked in the strongest terms Palmerston's defence of Don Pacifico's claims, just as they disapproved of his aggressions against China. Both attacked the expense involved in Palmerston's active policies, Disraeli more openly as spokesman for the opposition, Gladstone perhaps more effectively when he was Palmerston's Chancellor of the Exchequer. Both also stressed the need for Britain to co-operate with the other European powers, especially France, if war in Europe was to be avoided. Their sane attitude to France, revealed during the war scare of 1860 when both men urged moderation on Palmerston, was to be one theme on which the two rivals never clashed.

In his Guildhall speech of 1879 Disraeli outlined the principles upon which he had acted. He stressed the combination of 'Imperium et Libertas', of Britain's duty as the wealthiest of empires to honour her obligations to Europe. 'So long as the power and advice of England are felt in the councils of Europe, peace, I believe, will be maintained, and for a long period.' Despite his flirtation with imperialism Disraeli recognised Britain's decisive rôle in Europe. Indeed when Disraeli spoke of Empire he did not mean merely colonial annexations, but the whole power of Britain, which was based on both her territorial possessions and her moral influence in the world. Gladstone in his Midlothian campaign summed up his attitude to Britain's part in international relations in much the same way. He sought to strengthen and use the Empire to preserve 'the blessings of peace' by enabling Britain to play her part in European affairs, acknowledging the

[1]For a discussion of Palmerston's policy see: D. R. Ward, *Foreign Affairs 1815-1865*, in this series.

rights of all nations, avoiding 'needless and entangling engagements' which undermined Britain's freedom of action and reduced the power of the Empire.

The conflict over foreign affairs arose out of their different interpretation of the same principles, a difference of approach which was clear, before either of them became Prime Minister, in their attitudes to Italy. Disraeli criticised Liberalism for its alien roots, but it did at least provide Gladstone with an understanding of nineteenth-century nationalist movements, an understanding which Disraeli's belief in aristocratic government prevented him from achieving. For Disraeli Habsburg rule in Italy was right and proper, because hallowed by tradition, but Gladstone saw in Austrian domination the obstacle to the Italians' right to govern themselves. Such a lack of sympathy on Disraeli's part was to affect his policy adversely, not least in his lack of concern for the Balkan peoples. Yet at the same time, though Gladstone's attitude has earned more approval, it too was a weakness on occasions. The expansion of the European empires, including that of Britain, came into conflict with aspiring nationalist movements, and Gladstone's policies, torn between duty to preserve Britain's interests and personal sympathy with nationalism, seemed hesitant and ineffective. Gladstone saw too many sides to the problems of diplomacy, which tended to make him irresolute, whereas Disraeli saw too few, which tended to make him imprudent.

2 Gladstone, Disraeli and the Great Powers

Britain's policy of non-intervention in the affairs of Europe unless her interests were at stake was already well established before the death of Palmerston. The growing isolation that this policy involved was also evident, and Palmerston and Russell had had to retreat from their threatened interference over the Austro-Prussian seizure of Schleswig-Holstein when it became apparent that neither France nor any other European power would act with them. Even when a British interest was thought to be at stake, Britain had been condemned to isolation. The counterpart of isolation is isolated action, clearly illustrated by Gladstone's relations with the Great Powers during his first ministry.

The first task with which Gladstone and his Foreign Secretary, Lord Clarendon, had to deal was a seeming threat to Belgian neutrality, occasioned by the amalgamation of two Belgian railways with a French one. France was at once informed of Britain's determination to defend Belgian independence. The whole incident served merely to alarm Gladstone and deepen suspicions of Napoleon III, much to the Prussian Chancellor Bismarck's satisfaction. It also presented directly to Gladstone for the first time the problem he found so difficult to resolve: how to determine when British interests were so jeopardised by events as to warrant intervention, and how this intervention could be made effective. It emerged again almost immediately with the onset of the Franco-Prussian War.

It has been suggested that energetic action by Gladstone and Lord Granville, who had replaced Clarendon on the latter's death in 1870, could have averted the outbreak of war between France and Prussia. In fact Britain advised the Spanish government to abandon the Hohenzollern candidature for the Spanish throne, which had so alarmed France, and advised the French not to press for an official rejection of the candidature by the King of Prussia, which was to inflame German opinion. But France was determined to secure some sort of Prussian humiliation, even at the risk of declaring war, and thus played into Bismarck's hands. Britain could perhaps have prevented war, but only by committing herself to intervention on one side or the other, and to this public opinion was certainly opposed. It was also clear to Gladstone that Britain had not the military means at her disposal. When Bismarck released the Franco-Prussian draft treaty of 1866, which revealed Napoleon III's ambitions for Belgium, British public opinion became even more negative. The threat to Belgium, however, could not be ignored, and by August both belligerents had signed a treaty with Britain guaranteeing Belgian neutrality. An important British interest was successfully safeguarded. Gladstone's duty to preserve British interests and his sympathy for small nation states were on this occasion easily reconciled.

The defeat of France at Sedan and the German determination to annex Alsace-Lorraine won some sympathy for France, but Gladstone's attempt to persuade Bismarck to abandon his decision to take Alsace-Lorraine without a plebiscite was made not on behalf of France, but because Gladstone objected to the transfer of land without the consent of the inhabitants. Fortunately the Cabinet were not prepared to support him in this move, which served only to annoy Germany. Nevertheless Gladstone was undeniably correct in assuming that 'this violent laceration and transfer is to lead us from bad to worse, and to be the beginning of a new series of European complications'.

In October 1870 Russia denounced the clauses of the 1856 Treaty of Paris which had closed the Black Sea to Russian warships. The handling of this complication by Gladstone and Granville aroused the first criticisms and doubts about Liberal foreign policy. British public opinion became strongly anti-Russian, but with France prostrate even the Queen urged moderation. Discussions with Bismarck, in which the possibility of British action against Russia was threatened, led to his proposal of a European conference for the regulation of the Black Sea question. Granville insisted it should meet in London rather than St. Petersburg. The Treaty of London of 1871, though it left the Straits closed, removed the restrictions on Russia in the Black Sea, a clear set-back for British interests. However, Granville attempted to save face by including in the treaty 'the essential principle of the law of nations', that treaties could not be abrogated without the consent of all the signatories. To this Russia agreed. Though both Granville and Gladstone appeared weak and ineffective at the time, A. J. P. Taylor has argued that, having signed the treaty of 1871, Russia was willing seven years later to submit the Treaty of San Stefano to international examination at the Congress of Berlin, and that peace was therefore due partly to the despised London Conference.

Gladstone had asserted the rule of international law at the London Conference, and did so again in settling the 'Alabama' Question in 1872. The one important action taken in the field of foreign affairs by Disraeli's brief first ministry in 1868 was

Lord Stanley's decision to commit Britain to arbitration on the vexed dispute of the 'Alabama' claims. The Americans were claiming compensation for the damage caused by British-built ironclads such as the 'Alabama' in the Civil War—ironclads which the British government had failed to prevent sailing to the Confederate States. Granville was largely responsible for the negotiations, and in 1872 agreed to pay the Americans the £3,250,000 awarded by the arbitrators. The result was a steady improvement in Anglo-American relations, but, at the same time, more doubts were expressed about Liberal weakness in foreign policy. 1872 was the year Disraeli began to prepare for the next election, and part of his campaign was a policy of assertion in foreign affairs. Disraeli caught the mood of a large section of public opinion when he declared; 'It would have been better for us all if there had been a little more energy in our foreign policy, and a little less in our domestic legislation.'

France's defeat in 1870 left Germany paramount on the Continent, with Austria-Hungary eager to become her ally. Bismarck had secured Russian neutrality in the years before 1870, and he now sought to bring the emperors of the three Eastern powers together in a *Dreikaiserbund* (Three Emperors' League) and, by isolating France, prevent her from reversing the outcome of the Franco-Prussian War. Britain's policy of non-intervention, which Gladstone had followed, emphasised Britain's isolation and assisted Bismarck. When Disraeli became Prime Minister in 1874, he was determined to avoid Gladstone's timidity in foreign affairs and assert Britain's influence in the world. Such an active foreign policy was not only good politics, but appealed to the eccentric and romantic aspirations of Disraeli's ambitions. In Europe he sought to create a breach between the Eastern Powers—an important factor in his handling of the Eastern Question between 1875 and 1878. Yet if Disraeli, unlike Gladstone, refused to turn his back on a problem, he could not avoid the fact of Britain's isolation, and an isolated action would only succeed if it involved a threat of force.

The war scare of 1875, occasioned by an article in a German newspaper on French rearmament under the heading 'Is War in

Sight?', led to a flurry of diplomatic activity. The scare soon subsided. In 1870 Britain alone had urged moderation on France and Prussia. The reason for success in 1875 was not the change from Gladstone to Disraeli, but that Russia and Austria-Hungary now urged moderation also. Furthermore Bismarck had only been flying a kite. The result in London was to encourage the view that he was a warmonger, a view that Bismarck was unable to dispel until the Congress of Berlin. R. W. Seton-Watson has pointed out that 'as his (Disraeli's) oriental blood has so often been cited as explaining his interest in Eastern affairs, it is necessary to insist that it was in the affairs of Western Europe that his vision was clearest and most consistent'. Disraeli both pursued a policy of friendship with France, repairing the damage caused by Palmerston, and avoided the mistake of Gladstone in underestimating the forces which were creating a German dominance in Central Europe.

The unification of Germany and Italy in 1870 and the defeat of France lessened the likelihood of conflict within Western Europe in that there was less room for the Great Powers to manoeuvre. However, the rivalries continued, particularly in the power vacuum created by the decline of the Ottoman Empire, and increasingly in the complexities of empire-building. The European chancelleries remained the centre of activity, but it was activity concerned with non-European developments.

3 The Bulgarian Crisis and the Eastern Question

The decline of the Ottoman Empire was hastened not only by the disintegration of Turkish administration within the empire, but also by the pressure of Austria-Hungary and particularly Russia from without. Both these European empires seemed to seek further expansion at the expense of Turkey as a justification for their own moribund autocratic regimes. An increasingly important factor in Turkey's decline was the growing national awareness of the Christian races in the Balkans, suffering under various degrees of Turkish misrule. This both exposed the chronic and intolerable government of the Turks, and provided Russia and Austria-Hungary with excuses for intervention. There were three possible solutions to the Eastern Question, which simply posed the problem of what was to happen to the Ottoman Empire. First Turkey could reform herself from within. Secondly, the Turkish Empire could be partitioned, with Russia and Austria-Hungary dividing the Balkan area between themselves, and France and Britain, and possible Italy, finding compensation in the African and Near Eastern parts of the empire. The third alternative was to set up independent nation states in the Balkans and the other parts of the empire where this was practicable. This last course, however, was not really considered in Britain before the agitation of 1876, although previously both Serbia and Roumania had virtually struggled free of Turkey.

Certainly Disraeli did not consider setting up nationalist states in the Balkans. He disliked nationalism as a radical force, for in most cases it was involved with the struggle for land reforms; and the expropriation of landlords, even though hatred of the landlord was disguised as hatred of the foreign oppressor, was repugnant to Disraeli's thinking. Russian expansion anywhere in the Near East was regarded as a threat to India, and was not a prospect that Britain could support. British foreign policy was, therefore, based on the idea of Turkey eventually reforming herself. This involved Britain in attempting to hold the ring, in order to give Turkey time to reform. Gladstone suggested that Disraeli's attempt to bolster up Turkey was motivated by racial bias, exerted through the latter's contacts with the pro-Turkish Jewish community in Europe. It is more likely, however, that Disraeli accepted the traditional standpoint of British foreign policy firmly established by Palmerston.

The problem of the Christian subjects of the Turk produced an international crisis in 1875 when the Turkish provinces of Bosnia and Herzegovina rebelled. Their declared aim was to seek union with the South Slav states of Serbia and Montenegro, two vassal states of Turkey, but with considerable independence. There was the added danger that the rebellion would spread eastwards to the Bulgars. Austria-Hungary could not ignore the situation so near her southern borders, and was anxious that Russia should not take the initiative. Andrassy, the Austro-

Hungarian Foreign Secretary, and the Russian ambassador in Vienna produced the Andrassy Note, which urged the Turks to promise land reforms in Bosnia and Herzegovina. What was Disraeli's policy in this new crisis?

Disraeli was at first reluctant to agree to the Note, for in granting rights to the Bosnian peasants it might encourage the Irish peasants. But in December 1875 all the powers, including Turkey, accepted the Note. Austria-Hungary and Britain were anxious to localise the rebellion and prevent Russian interference. Bismarck in Germany played a less obvious game. He was attempting to prove to Russia the value of German support, hoping eventually to secure Russia as an ally against France. An understanding between Germany and Austria-Hungary had already been secured and Bismarck's plan was to extend this into the *Dreikaiserbund*. His task was to avoid a conflict between Russia and Austria-Hungary in case either should ally with France, and he hoped, therefore, that a realistic balance would be maintained in the Balkans. Disraeli and his Foreign Secretary, Lord Derby, wanted to avoid a settlement by the three Eastern Powers which did not take account of British interests. Austria-Hungary, perhaps feeling neglected as Bismarck courted Russia, acted with Britain in pressing the Sultan to embark on internal reform. The Turks were offended by this European intervention, but the Eastern Powers, on Andrassy's initiative, now produced the Berlin Memorandum, which called upon Turkey to conclude an armistice with the rebels for two months and carry out reforms. Disraeli rejected the Berlin proposals. He was anxious to develop a more independent policy.

Although the Memorandum contained suggestions for reform in line with British policy, Disraeli was not prepared to trust Bismarck or Gortchakov, the Russian Foreign Minister who had tricked England over the Black Sea clauses in 1871. The Memorandum contained the implication, inserted by Gortchakov, of possible action by the Powers if the armistice failed. This hint of coercing the Turks ensured its rejection by Disraeli. Rejection provided Disraeli with the opportunity of striking at the emergent *Dreikaiserbund* and asserting British independence of action.

The British Mediterranean fleet was ordered to Besika Bay as the first sign of this new independence, but the effect, with the rejection of the Berlin Memorandum, was to encourage the intransigence of the Turks, who felt sure Britain would protect them from aggression. Britain's independent actions did not succeed. At the beginning of July 1876 Serbia and Montenegro, with armies largely commanded by Russian officers, declared war on Turkey. At Reichstadt Tsar Alexander II and the Emperor Francis Joseph met to partition the Balkans. Serbia, however, was heavily defeated, and the succession of the new Sultan, Abdul Hamid, the last of three sultans to appear in 1876, led to the withdrawal of the Berlin Memorandum—which Disraeli saw as justifying Britain's rejection.

The whole issue was further complicated by the revolt of the Bulgars in May 1876, and the ensuing wholesale massacre of the rebels by the Turkish Bashi-Bazouks. Disraeli at once appreciated that the revolt in Bulgaria, bordering the Black Sea and therefore open to Russian access, was a far more serious threat to British interests centred in the Turkish Empire than the rebellion in Bosnia-Herzegovina, which looked towards Austria-Hungary for help. But for the moment he was unable to act.

When the news of the Bulgarian massacres began to appear during June in the Liberal *Daily News*, Disraeli, who relied heavily for information on Britain's pro-Turkish ambassador to Constantinople, Sir Henry Elliot, declared that the atrocities were 'to a large extent inventions' and 'coffee-house babble'. When official reports at last confirmed the massacres, Disraeli realised that events in Bulgaria had 'completely destroyed sympathy with Turkey', and made a British declaration of war against Russia if she intervened 'practically impossible'. Such a state of affairs was confirmed by the intervention of Gladstone with his pamphlet *The Bulgarian Horrors and the Question of the East*, which he had written in three days whilst in bed with lumbago. Gladstone argued for British non-intervention, believing this would assist the Christians: 'Let the Turks now carry away their abuses in the only possible way, namely by carrying off themselves . . . one and all, bag and baggage . . . There is not a criminal in a European gaol, there is not a cannibal in the South Sea Islands whose indignation would not arise and overboil at the recital of that which has been done.' Disraeli saw such a point of view would lead to further Russian penetration in the Balkans and along the Black Sea coast. He dismissed the pamphlet as 'vindictive and ill-written', and argued that it was the work of 'designing politicians . . . for the furtherance of sinister ends'.

Gladstone's campaign in the autumn of 1876 sabotaged Disraeli's policy. By dividing British public opinion and sanctifying Russia's pretext for intervention, Gladstone effectively destroyed Disraeli's freedom of action. Lord Salisbury was sent as British delegate to the Constantinople Conference, which recommended an armistice with the Serbs and a programme of reforms for Turkey—all with Russia's agreement. The Turks, however, would not accept, believing that Russia would shrink from war, and that Salisbury's threat to leave Turkey to her fate was an idle one. This was largely Disraeli's fault in refusing Salisbury's request to remove the pro-Turkish Elliot from Constantinople. Discussions were continued and another protocol was issued, but Turkey obdurately refused to give way. In April 1877 Russia declared war on Turkey. Disraeli declared Britain's neutrality, though warning Russia of the inviolability of Constantinople and the navigation of the Straits, and added to these old demands the maintenance of free communication through the Suez Canal and the exclusion of Egypt from military operations. The effect of Gladstone's intervention in weakening Disraeli's hand cannot be denied, but why did he intervene?

John Morley, writing on Gladstone before the First World War, saw in his agitation of 1876 a sympathy with the inalienable rights of smaller nations to their nationhood, whilst Sir Robert Ensor and R. W. Seton-Watson, writing in the 1930s, gave Gladstone credit for realising what by 1935 seemed to be the solution to the containment of Russia, the setting up of independent states in the Balkans. The presence of Russian satellite states in the Balkans by 1946, following the eclipse of Germany, would seem to indicate that Disraeli was perhaps correct in his distrust of the ability of Balkan states to thwart the ambitions of Russia on their own. Moreover in *Gladstone and the Bulgarian Agitation* R. T. Shannon has shed new light on the part played by Gladstone. Shannon emphasises that Gladstone did not join the agitation until September, over two months after it had been launched by Nonconformist elements in the Liberal party. Furthermore Gladstone sought to restrict the growth of the movement; he was not seeking to change Britain's policy in the Near East, and quietly accepted Turkish territorial integrity. It was 'less a case of Gladstone exciting popular passion, than popular passion exciting Gladstone'. Gladstone was more concerned with attacking the Conservative government, which was the supporter of the Turkish Empire and therefore its accomplice in the massacres, than with attacking the atrocities themselves. Certainly Disraeli regarded Gladstone as worse than any Bulgarian horror. Shannon's view seems to agree more with Gladstone's policies when he became Prime Minister again, and strengthens the growing impression of recent research into other aspects of Gladstone's career, that Gladstone the politician lurked not far below the surface of Gladstone the man of principle.

The popularity of Gladstone's attack on the Turks did not last long, and Disraeli was able to resume his policy. The outbreak of war between Turkey and Russia led to a revival of anti-Russian feelings in Britain and public opinion began to swing back behind Disraeli. Disraeli would have occupied the Dardanelles at once, had not Derby, Salisbury and Carnarvon dissuaded him, but in January 1878 he ordered the British Mediterranean fleet through the Dardanelles to Constantinople, and at the same time asked Parliament for £6 million for military purposes. At Adrianople the Russians, themselves exhausted, granted the Turks an armistice. In February Russia undertook not to occupy the peninsula on which Constantinople stood if Britain did not land troops in Turkey, and in March Russia and Turkey signed the Treaty of San Stefano. The war ended, but an international crisis flared up again.

The Treaty of San Stefano was clearly intended to ensure Russian domination of the Balkans. By the creation of what was called Big Bulgaria, stretching southwards from Roumania to the Aegean Sea and westwards from the Black Sea to Serbia, and including Macedonia with its Greek and Serb populations, Russia attempted to leave Turkey nothing but northern Greece on the mainland, cut off from the rest of the Turkish Empire by the intrusion of Bulgaria southwards to the sea. At the same time the expansion of Serbia south and east would be prevented, whilst Austro-Hungarian ambitions eastwards to the Black Sea would also be blocked by Big Bulgaria. Big Bulgaria itself was seen simply as a Russian satellite, which would allow Russia both to dominate the Balkans and threaten Constantinople. At the same time the Russo-Turkish frontier in Asia Minor was advanced fifty miles along the Black Sea coast and up to a hundred miles inland. Russian interests in the Straits were also to be safeguarded. As Ensor has remarked, 'Russia made war in the name of liberty; she made peace in the spirit of annexation.' Britain and Austria-Hungary at once protested and called for a European conference, for the Treaty of San Stefano involved a profound change in the European balance of power.

When Russia vacillated about the scope of the conference, Disraeli called up the British reserves and sent to the Mediterranean a large body of Indian troops. Lord Derby, the Foreign Secretary and son of Disraeli's former leader, who disagreed with the decision because he believed a negotiated peace was only possible if Britain remained neutral, and disapproved of Disraeli's bidding for Cyprus, resigned. Since 1875 Derby had accepted the Russian claim that they merely sought reforms and not the dissolution of the Turkish Empire, and he believed the real danger of a European war to lie in bellicose statements by the British government. He was, therefore, increasingly opposed to Disraeli's desire for action, even to the extent of informing the Russian ambassador in London of the division in the British Cabinet, hoping that peace would be preserved. In the Cabinet Derby put his foot down against any action that implied war, so that long before his resignation Disraeli was attempting to run foreign policy behind his back. Blake disagrees with Seton-Watson over the interpretation of Disraeli's warlike actions throughout the Eastern crisis, suggesting that Disraeli believed peace could be preserved only by the threat of war, rather than that he deliberately sought to pick a quarrel. Certainly at the time Lord Derby was concerned over Disraeli's bellicose actions, and by 1880 he had joined the Liberal party.

The immediate issue by Salisbury of a Circular Note to the European powers, and pressure exerted by Austria-Hungary, brought Bismarck down from the fence in favour of an unlimited conference. Russia, in financial difficulties and with Ignatiev visibly losing influence, agreed. The Congress of Berlin finally brought Disraeli's policy to fruition.

The success of the Congress for the Great Powers was largely assured by secret conventions concluded beforehand, which then appeared in the Treaty of Berlin. Big Bulgaria, the main bone of contention, was divided into three parts. Macedonia was returned to Turkey without a Christian governor, and provided a land link between northern Greece, which was still part of the Turkish Empire, and Constantinople. Between Macedonia and what was to be a smaller Bulgaria, the new Turkish province of Eastern Roumelia was established under a Christian governor. This left in the north the new Bulgaria, which was to be a vassal state of Turkey ruled over by a freely elected Christian prince. The Turks were to garrison the frontier between Bulgaria and Eastern Roumelia, thus being provided with the Balkan Mountains as a defensible frontier. Britain accepted the annexation by Russia of Batum and Kars in Asia, and in return Russia agreed to make no further advance and to surrender Bayazid, which had given her control of the Trebizond-Tabriz caravan route. Disraeli had hoped for more concessions from Russia, but Salisbury was satisfied that they had been successful enough in controlling Russian ambitions, and Disraeli did not press the matter.

To what extent was the Treaty of Berlin a success for Disraeli? Disraeli had succeeded in fending off the Russian threat to the Turkish Empire; he had secured his 'peace with honour', and his personal standing was enhanced both at home and abroad, many agreeing with Bismarck's remark, *'Der alte Jude, das ist der Mann.'* In addition to defending British interests in the Near

RUSSIA

BESSARABIA

AUSTRIA–HUNGARY

ROUMANIA

DOBRUJA

HERZEGOVINA

BOSNIA

SERBIA

BULGARIA

BLACK SEA

MONTE-
NEGRO

EASTERN ROUMELIA

Constantinople

Salonika

DARDANELLES

BESIKA BAY

IONIAN ISLANDS

GREECE

——— Bulgaria at San Stefano

Turkish Empire 1878

Bosnia-Herzegovina to be administered by Austria–Hungary
by Treaty of Berlin

EASTERN QUESTION 1876-1878

East, Disraeli also claimed credit for destroying the *Dreikaiser-bund*. Bismarck's balance had been secured in the Balkans, but Russia had wanted domination, and Bismarck was partly blamed by the Russians for their failure. There was a temporary rift between Berlin and St. Petersburg, but only until 1881. More significantly Austria-Hungary drew closer to Germany, and became more subservient to German ambitions. A. J. P. Taylor has argued that, with the signing of the Treaty of Berlin in 1878, Turkey realised that her protector had failed to protect her, and that the origin of the Berlin-Baghdad axis is to be found in the Congress of Berlin rather than the occupation of Egypt in 1882. Nevertheless Britain obtained the destruction of Big Bulgaria without a formal ally and without war. For some commentators this was a hollow triumph, for Bulgaria was never to be subservient to Russia, as had been feared. Big Bulgaria, however, with large Serb and Greek minorities, might well have fallen into dependence on Russia. Blake concludes that the Treaty of Berlin 'was followed by almost as long a period of peace between the European great powers as the interval separating the Crimean War from the Congress of Vienna. As one of the two principal plenipotentiaries at Berlin Disraeli must share with Bismarck some part of the credit.'

Apart from the satisfaction of having peacefully solved the Bulgarian crisis, Disraeli also acquired Cyprus for Britain in a secret Anglo-Turkish Convention made before the Berlin conference. Gladstone had been forced to agree that the Congress of Berlin appeared a success, but he denounced the Cyprus agreement. It was this attack that brought from Disraeli his most bitter denunciation of Gladstone as 'a sophisticated rhetorician, inebriated with the exuberance of his own verbosity, and gifted with an egotistical imagination that can at all times command an interminable and inconsistent series of arguments to malign an opponent and glorify himself'. Britain also signed a defensive alliance with Turkey, promising to defend Turkey-in-Asia in return for the Sultan's pledge to introduce reforms and to protect his Christian subjects in consultation with Britain. Disraeli seems to have been considering friendly British penetration through to the Persian Gulf and India with Cyprus as a base. Salisbury arranged also to send British military consuls to Armenia to organise Turkey's frontier defences. The only power to protest at these arrangements was France, but she was appeased by Britain's secret consent to her seizure of Tunis, which took place in 1881.

The Congress of Berlin restored Disraeli's personal prestige, but the massacres of Isandhlwana and Kabul revived Gladstone's attack, and Disraeli was ousted from office in 1880. The attempt to bolster up Turkey was at once abandoned. Gladstone withdrew the military consuls from Armenia, and so paved the way for German military advice to Turkey, and he brought pressure on Turkey to fulfil the promises of territorial concession made to Greece and Montenegro at the Congress of Berlin. He did not return Cyprus, because neither the inhabitants of the island nor the Turks wished it returned, though the occupation of Egypt authorised by Gladstone made the base superfluous. However, Gladstone had no plan for the dismemberment of the Turkish Empire, for that could involve war with either France or Russia, and he did not want that.

Yet despite all the activity the Eastern Question remained. The Congress of Berlin failed either to revive the Ottoman Empire as an independent power or to partition it—the question of what would happen to that Empire was still to be answered.

4 Afghanistan Fear of Russia and a more direct threat to India occasioned Britain's interest in Afghanistan. However, Lord Salisbury was the first to suggest that the importance of Afghanistan in British imperial strategy was misplaced. The Foreign Office saw Afghanistan on its maps as a buffer state between Russia and India, and therefore stressed the need for Britain to safeguard the area without realising that the deserts and mountain ranges made the country impassable to a large invasion force. Presumably the Russian Foreign Office made the same mistake, for Russia certainly seemed anxious to bring Afghanistan within her sphere of influence. In fairness it should be pointed out that throughout history Afghanistan had been the base from which northern conquerors invaded India. Whether the Russians in Afghanistan were a real threat to India is unimportant; what is important is that Britain thought them to be, and acted accordingly.

Palmerston had first authorised intervention in Afghanistan in 1839 in order to stop the possible advance of Russia to the North-west frontier approaches of India. Though the Russians were ousted, that adventure had resulted in retreat and disaster in 1842. A revival of this 'forward' policy took place when Disraeli appointed Lord Lytton as Viceroy in India in 1875. Disraeli was incapable of following a policy of inactivity. The Queen was about to be proclaimed Empress of India as a sign of Britain's determination to hold on to India, and as a warning to the Russians. Disraeli was concerned about the possible Russian invasion of Afghanistan, and Lytton was instructed to induce Sher Ali, the Amir of Afghanistan, to receive a friendly British mission in the country. Offers of a subsidy and material assistance against unprovoked aggression were also to be made. As a first step the Treaty of Jacobabad was signed in 1876 with the Khan of Kalat, which enabled British troops to use the town of Quetta as a base for striking at Kandahar in southern Afghanistan. Sher Ali, however, had been making military preparations on a vast scale with Russian assistance since 1873. He refused to admit British agents to discuss a treaty in 1876, and when a meeting was held at Peshwar in 1877 Sher Ali refused the British terms. A Russian mission appeared in Kabul, the capital city, in 1878, and when a British mission was still refused, Lytton sent an ultimatum, which the Amir ignored. Despite instructions to proceed with caution Lytton, who took the view that Sher Ali was an unreliable savage, ordered three British armies into Afghanistan. Russia, more concerned with her interests in the Balkans at this time, did not offer help, and Sher Ali fled. Yahut Khan succeeded his father, and signed in 1879 the Treaty of Gandamak, ceding to Britain military control over the passes to India, accepting British control of foreign policy and agreeing to the presence of a British envoy at Kabul. The alarm occasioned by Lytton's action subsided as his policy brought success, and Disraeli refrained from expressing his disapproval of Lytton's disobedience. In September 1879, however, the British Legation at Kabul, including the envoy, Cavagnari, was massacred. The Amir fled to the British at Kandahar as civil war broke out. Lytton now planned to partition Afghanistan, Britain controlling the south from Kandahar, but with the change of government at home Lytton was replaced in 1880 by Lord Ripon, who abandoned the plan of partition. The idea of Afghanistan as a buffer state was revived.

Disraeli's image had improved after the Treaty of Berlin, but the Kabul massacre reminded many of the excessive amount Disraeli had paid for the Suez Canal shares, the useless and flamboyant gesture of the Royal Titles Act, and his insensitivity to the Bulgarian massacres. The Afghan War persuaded the Liberals to make the government's foreign and imperial policy their main object of attack. In some ways Kabul was Disraeli's Khartoum. Lord Salisbury blamed Disraeli for not taking a stronger line with Lytton, though, as Gladstone found with Gordon, it was difficult to dictate to 'the man on the spot' when long distances and primitive communications were involved. The government's adventures at the expense of an independent state had resulted in disaster, and Kabul was heavy ammunition for Gladstone in his Midlothian campaigns: 'Remember the rights of the savage. Remember that the happiness of his humble home, remember that the sanctity of life in the hill villages of Afghanistan, among the winter snows, is as inviolable in the eyes of Almighty God as can be your own.'

On becoming Prime Minister again Gladstone reversed Disraeli's forward policy in Afghanistan by withdrawing the British garrison from Kandahar. The government recognised the sovereignty of the new Amir, Abdur Rahman, and Britain withdrew her claim to a resident envoy. Assistance to the Amir in crushing the rebellion restored British prestige in the area, and led to the establishment of friendly relations between the two countries, though Britain did not have the closer control that Disraeli had advocated. Even so this successful withdrawal from

Afghanistan was regarded by many as another example of Liberal weakness. The Penjdeh incident in 1885, however, upset this point of view.

By 1885 Anglo-Russian negotiations over the boundary between Afghanistan and Russia, which Gladstone had initiated, had reached deadlock. The news from Khartoum had already shaken the Liberal government, and the Russians decided that whilst British attention was centred on the Nile, they would make their move along the Oxus. Britain tried unsuccessfully to restrain the Afghans, but at Penjdeh fighting broke out, and the Russians forced the Afghans to retreat. Perhaps Gladstone wished to deflect attention away from the Sudan, or perhaps he had temporarily lost the nerve to fly in the face of public opinion, but he announced to the House of Commons that the attack bore 'the appearance of unprovoked aggression', and the Cabinet actually drafted a declaration of war against Russia. The unexpected development of Gladstone as a warmonger surprised the Russians, who immediately withdrew from Afghanistan. Fortunately the Amir let the matter go, and Gladstone's desire to uphold the dignity and prestige of Britain was assuaged by the revival of the Boundary Commission. Gladstone seemed prepared to act more decisively because it was a clear case of aggression. He no more approved of Russia's attempt to overawe Afghanistan than he did of Disraeli's.

5 Expansion in Africa   At the beginning of the 1870s Britain had a few settlements, little more than trading stations, along the west coast of Africa, plus Cape Colony and Natal, much more important strategically as guarding the sea route to India and the Pacific. Further expansion was not envisaged. Gladstone in criticising the purchase of Suez Canal shares may have had a sudden insight: 'Our first site in Egypt, be it by larceny or be it by eruption, will be the almost certain egg of a North African Empire that will grow and grow till we finally join hands across the equator with Natal and Cape Town.' However, Disraeli dismissed the idea of a British occupation of Egypt as 'moonshine', and Gladstone himself could be relied on not to embark

on a policy of expansion. Even Lord Salisbury, a less obvious critic of imperial ambitions, admitted in 1880, 'Nobody thought about Africa.' Yet by the 1890s a British Empire was firmly established in Africa. Robinson and Gallagher have pointed out that 'the statesmen who drew the new frontier lines did not do so because they wanted to rule and develop these countries . . . the chief partitioners of the 1880s glimpsed no grand imperial idea behind what they were doing . . . the partition of Africa is a remarkable freak'. How then did Britain come to rule an African empire? Three general theories have been advanced and need to be examined.

The first detailed explanation was offered by John Hobson in his book *Imperialism*, published in 1902. Hobson dismissed the 'official' explanations of commerce and Christianity by pointing out that British trade with Africa was small compared to her trade with industrial nations in Europe and America. He argued, however, that the new territorial gains in Africa did benefit a small group of capitalists, those investing in shipping and armaments, and it was this small group of investors who played on jingoistic sentiments to encourage expansion in Africa and elsewhere in the tropics. Lenin in his pamphlet *Imperialism, the Highest Stage of Capitalism* refined Hobson's argument, and as 'neo-colonialism' the explanation remains a thesis used to account for European interest in Africa. Certainly private European trading companies were often the first to move into large areas of Africa, to be followed later by the European governments. Although the activities of the African companies were an embarrassment to the British government, and often forged further ahead than the government wanted them to, they were never regarded as the enemies of the overall policy of expansion that developed. British governments excused their annexations as attempts to protect British settlers, but the result was also to protect British capital investments in the annexed areas. Yet if African trade represented such a small part of the British economy why did successive British governments feel obliged to intervene? There is no evidence to indicate any direct pressure from scheming capitalists. It is even possible to argue that Liberal and Conservative governments in Britain encouraged private companies in the first place in order to secure occupation 'on the cheap'. It is certainly difficult to envisage Parliament granting money for such an activity until the value of the territory had been established.

The explanation offered by many historians in the inter-war period was linked to a general theory to account for the outbreak of the First World War. They saw the rivalries of the European powers transferred from Europe to Africa, so that the battle to maintain or disrupt the European balance of power was fought in an African arena. This explanation seems to fit the paper division of Africa by the Great Powers, but it does not fully explain why the paper empires of the 1880s became the real territorial empires, why the diplomatic game resulted in imperial occupation. Perhaps capitalist exploitation provides the answer. But more recently a new explanation has been offered.

The Robinson-Gallagher thesis advanced in *Africa and the Victorians* argues that Britain's increasing involvement in Africa was in fact not the result of any interest in Africa itself, that Britain's territorial claims in Africa were 'little more than by-products of an enforced search for better security in the Mediterranean and the East'. The motive for intervention in Egypt was to protect the main trade route to India and the Pacific, whilst the rise of the Boers in their independent republics threatened British control of the old Cape route to India and the Pacific. Furthermore, having intervened in Africa, a new momentum was given to further intervention by 'nationalist crises in Africa itself'. The rise of Islamic nationalism in the north and Afrikaner sentiment in the south drew Britain further into Africa. Expansion in South Africa and Egypt was not set off by new imperial ambitions; 'In both the late Victorians, striving to uphold an old system of paramountcy against a nationalist challenge, fell almost involuntarily into conquering and occupying more territory.' From these early nationalist struggles Robinson and Gallagher claim the modern struggles against foreign rule were later to emerge. Writing in 1961 they demonstrate the truth of Croce's remark that 'all history is contemporary history'. Aware of the existence of modern independent African states, both north and south of the Sahara, Robinson and Gallagher offer an explanation of late-nineteenth-century history which has added meaning in the light of contemporary developments in Arab and African nationalism. But did Disraeli, Gladstone and Salisbury think in these terms? The threat to India came from Russia, and that focused attention on Constantinople and the North-West Frontier.

These theories tend to contradict each other in offering an explanation of expansion in Africa. To what extent do the imperial policies of Disraeli and Gladstone support such theories, particularly with regard to Egypt and South Africa?

An analysis of Britain's concern with Egypt in this period raises some important questions. What was Britain's interest in Egypt? How wise was Disraeli to buy shares in the Suez Canal, and did this increasing financial interest lead automatically to occupation? Why did Gladstone feel compelled to crush the Arabi revolt, and why did Britain fail before 1914 to keep her frequent promises to withdraw from Egypt?

British business interests, expecting failure, kept aloof from the French Suez Canal Company, but when the Canal opened in 1869 it proved increasingly successful and profitable, whilst such a sea-link to India was a necessary concern for Britain. With the possible threat of French control or Russian intervention it became a vital concern. The Canal added to the importance of Egypt in British imperial strategy, for already in 1815 and 1840 Britain had tried to expel France from Egypt, though without establishing herself there. France was the main rival in Egypt, but if Britain had seized Egypt unequivocally nothing would have stopped a mass partition of the Turkish Empire, which would inevitably have increased the Russian menace both to the eastern Mediterranean and to India. Thus Britain was intensely interested in the area, and, at the same time, most reluctant to establish a firm base there.

When in 1875 the debt-ridden Khedive Ismail was forced to sell his holdings of Suez Canal Company shares, Disraeli at once appreciated the possibilities of purchasing the shares, persuaded Lord Derby on the matter, and together they secured the Cabinet's consent. Four million pounds had to be found immediately before the French government had time to buy. The money was not in the Treasury and Parliament was in summer recess, so Disraeli approached the financial house of Rothschilds, who at once advanced the money at a reasonable rate. The purchase gave Britain forty-five per cent of the total share capital, which, though not a majority of shares, Disraeli believed gave Britain 'an immense, not to say preponderating, influence in the management of the Canal'. Ismail was forced to admit Egypt's bankruptcy in 1876, and to hand over control of his country's finances to an international office, the 'Caisse de la Dette', directed by two controller-generals. Finally in 1879 Ismail was deposed for attempting to re-establish his financial control. It was only in 1879 that Britain agreed to appoint one of the controller-generals, and Sir Evelyn Baring, later Lord Cromer, was given the task. Financial considerations necessitated further responsibility.

Disraeli was the first to realise that the Canal transferred to Egypt most of the strategic importance which previously attached to the Cape of Good Hope. The Khedive had suggested in 1870 that the British Liberal government should buy his shares in what was then a non-paying concern, but his proposal had been rejected by the Foreign Office. Even in 1875 the Foreign Office had not taken the matter seriously, and it was Disraeli's initiative that secured the shares. It is possible, as Buckle has suggested, that Disraeli was partly prepared for the announcement to sell by the Rothschilds. However, the decision to purchase was Disraeli's. Was it a wise move, or was Gladstone right to denounce the purchase as one of Disraeli's 'mischievous and ruinous misdeeds' which meant that 'we have assumed jointly with France the virtual government of Egypt'?

The effect of the purchase throughout Europe was profound; it seemed as if Britain was abandoning her passive attitude and embarking on a more spirited policy. Bismarck was pleased, for he saw it as a first step to intervention in Egypt and conflict between Britain and France. Disraeli was aware of that danger and determined to avoid it. Yet the importance of Disraeli's action ought not to be exaggerated. It gave Britain some say in financial affairs, but not political or strategic control, for she had only three seats on the council of twenty-four members which managed the canal. A. J. P. Taylor has even argued that it was important for the future only in that it allowed British public opinion to tolerate Gladstone's occupation of Egypt later. How did Gladstone come to authorise the occupation of Egypt?

The Egyptian crisis which faced Gladstone was precipitated by a nationalist revolt at the end of 1881 which was directed against foreigners and led by Colonel Arabi. The Egyptians objected particularly to the 'Capitulations'—privileges, such as exemption from tax and the right to their own courts, granted to Europeans in the late Middle Ages in order to encourage trade. In addition they disliked the virtual monopoly of administrative posts by Turks and Armenians, whilst the Egyptian peasants groaned under the abuses of a gross feudal system. At the same time an Islamic revival encouraged hatred of the infidel. Egyptian army officers provided leadership for the revolution when their pay was cut by half as a result of Ismail's financial mismanagement. Here indeed was a nation struggling to be free, but it soon became clear that Arabi intended to repudiate all Egypt's foreign debts, whilst his attempt to fortify Alexandria was regarded as a deliberate threat to the British navy. These factors and the bankruptcy of Egypt shocked Gladstone out of any sympathy for the Egyptian nationalist movement. Gladstone was reluctant to take action, but his first priority was to protect British interests, and he now accepted the fact the Suez Canal was of immediate strategic importance to the Empire, vital for British shipping in the world's carrying trade. The nationalist revolt of the Egyptians threatened the safety of the route to India by threatening the informal control of Egypt by Britain and France. The alternative solution was conquest and rule. It was much the same conclusion that Sir Anthony Eden reached in 1956, but the intervention of 1882 was not a planned step; it became a necessary step for an unwilling government, dictated by the security of the Empire.

The problem was also international, and Gladstone suggested joint British and French intervention in the name of the Concert of Europe, though he had refused to countenance such a move when first suggested by the French Premier Gambetta. The British and French fleets arrived at Alexandria, but when it became clear that this naval show of strength would need to be followed by a military show of strength on land, the French, now led by Freycinet, who was attempting to negotiate with Arabi, withdrew. France had troops already in Tunis and Algeria, and to most Frenchmen the Suez Canal and trade with Egypt hardly seemed vital national interests. Heavy involvement in Egypt might distract French resources from the Rhine and the recovery of Alsace-Lorraine, the only objective for which there was truly national support in France. Italy and Germany, however, were prepared to support independent British action, but not to provide military help. Italy hoped Britain would support her in seeking compensation in North Africa, whilst Bismarck was prepared to support any action that would divide France from Britain. Thus Gladstone authorised the bombardment of Alexandria and the seizure of the Canal, and though Bright resigned in protest, Gladstone believed he had acted correctly, informing the House of Commons that 'we should not fully discharge our duty if we did not endeavour to convert the present interior state of Egypt from anarchy and conflict to peace and order'. In August 1882 Sir Garnet Wolseley landed at Port Said with an expeditionary force, Arabi was defeated at Tel-el-Kebir and banished, and the British Army occupied Egypt. Gladstone now faced the dilemma of whether to remain in occupation of Egypt or leave the country in hopeless disorder. He attempted to do neither.

Once the revolution in Egypt had been quashed, Gladstone soon discovered that the settlement of Egypt would be lengthy and expensive. As Lord Cromer has remarked in his study of Egypt, 'The army was in a state of mutiny; the treasury was bankrupt; every branch of the administration had been dislocated; the ancient and arbitrary methods under which the country had for centuries been governed had received a severe blow; whilst at the same time no more orderly and law-abiding form of government had been inaugurated to take its place.' It became clear that the British occupation would be a prolonged one. Gladstone has been accused of inconsistency in supporting nationalism in Ireland, in the Transvaal and even in the Sudan, but ignoring it in Egypt. However, there was evident proof for Gladstone that Egyptian nationalism would produce only chaos. It was the inevitability of chaos if he did not act which solved Gladstone's dilemma in that it prevented him from withdrawing from Egypt. In 1884 he defended himself in the House of Commons: 'I affirm, and will show, that the situation in Egypt is not one which we made, but one we found. I shall show that we never had any option.'

Gladstone attempted to place ultimate responsibility for the administration of Egypt in the hands of the Concert of Europe. In March 1885, after three years of negotiation, a Board of Control was established with Britain, France, Germany, Austria-Hungary, Russia and Italy having equal representation. The British Army remained however, and though Egypt was nominally a province of Turkey with its own Khedive and Egyptian ministers, real power was exercised by the British Agent and Consul-General, who until 1907 was Sir Evelyn Baring. This was perhaps a very practical way of strengthening a weak link in the Turkish Empire, but to many observers it seemed as if Britain had in fact acquired her share of the partition of the Turkish Empire without any compensation to France or Russia. As A. J. P. Taylor has pointed out, 'This was an extraordinary outcome, arrived at without plan or deliberation.' Britain's willingness to evacuate Egypt was frequently asserted, but it was dependent on the establishment of an Egyptian government which would be efficient, stable and pro-British. Such a government was not easy to create. Gladstone's conscience over the occupation seemed to live on after his death, for a total of sixty-six promises of withdrawal were made by Britain between 1882 and 1922.

One immediate result of the occupation of Egypt was that it dealt the final blow to the traditional friendship of Britain and Turkey, and the latter began to look for new friends. This in turn led to changing policies amongst the European powers.

Bismarck was prepared to play Turkey's game, for he saw in preserving the status quo in the Turkish Empire the way to preventing conflict between Austria-Hungary and Russia, the two powers he wished to ally with, but needed to reconcile to each other. The spring of 1882 saw the arrival of German officers to train and develop the Turkish army. In addition Russo-Turkish tension was relaxed, as Russia's hostility to Britain became a recommendation to the Turks. Thus during the Penjdeh crisis the *Dreikaiserbund* powers, at Russia's instigation, had no difficulty in persuading the Sultan to keep the Straits closed to British ships in the event of a Russo-British war. One unforeseen consequence of the occupation of Egypt was that Alexandria became a powerful British naval base, which removed gradually British concern over the Straits and Russian ambitions there. Britain's position in the eastern Mediterranean was no longer dependent on the closure of the Straits to Russian ships.

More dramatically the setting up of a Board of Control in Egypt lost Britain her diplomatic initiative. The French bitterly resented the position which Britain had acquired in a country which since the days of the Crusades had been a French sphere of influence. Russia was offended that Britain should move into the Turkish Empire, and yet resist Russian moves to do the same. Consequently Russia and France worked together on the Board of Control, and made British proposals for Egypt dependent on Germany and Austria-Hungary, who also co-operated with each other. Gladstone admitted the mistake to his electors in 1885; 'We have, according to my conviction, from the very first committed by our intervention in Egypt a grave political error ... Until we shall have been able to quit Egypt we shall ... remain liable in a hundred ways to be thwarted and humiliated through the numerous rights secured there, by international agreements, to other Powers.' Until 1914 Britain was prevented from exercising a free and detached influence on the groupings of the other powers. For this reason Ensor has argued that Gladstone ought to have annexed Egypt in 1882 and avoided the embarrassment of a Board of Control. A. J. P. Taylor, however, disagrees, for annexation would have precipitated a mass partition of the Turkish Empire and, as a possible consequence, a major European conflagration. Robinson and Gallagher have added to these arguments by insisting that 'from start to finish the partition of tropical Africa was driven by the persistent crisis in Egypt'. How acceptable is this last assertion?

There seems little doubt that Britain found it necessary to purchase German support for good government in Egypt with concessions in other parts of the world, including Africa. Britain acquiesced in the German annexation of South-West Africa, Togoland and the Cameroons, and in 1884 Gladstone accepted the rules for the further partition of Africa drawn up at the Berlin Conference. The most important decision was that no annexation or protectorate in Africa should be recognised unless it was made effective by the power claiming it. Such an agreement hardly coincided with Gladstone's ideas of self-determination announced in his election speeches. France may also have sought revenge for the loss of Egypt by expansion in West Africa, as Robinson and Gallagher argue, but Gladstone's first ministry had authorised an extension of British interests on the Gold Coast in 1873 long before the occupation of Egypt. Not only were the Dutch bought out in the area, but Sir Garnet Wolseley was sent to discipline the Ashanti, who were forced not only to abolish human sacrifice and the slave trade but also to abandon their claims to the coastal strip. French interests in West Africa may have increased after the occupation of Egypt and may have persuaded Gladstone to secure Britain's interests in Nigeria by setting up the Oil Rivers Protectorate in 1885, but British business interests clearly needed protection before as well as after the intervention in Egypt.

If Egypt was the natural springboard for all kinds of imperial adventure motivated by the need to protect the Suez route to India, then the obvious bastion to seize and hold was the Sudan. The opportunity arose in 1883 but was not taken up by the Liberal government. The rebellion of the Mahdi, a clear example of Islamic proto-nationalism, did not lead to annexation. What then was Gladstone's policy in 1883?

The Sudan, which had been under Egyptian rule for sixty years, took advantage of the Egyptian rebellion to have one of its own in 1883. Egypt's oppression and the abolition of the slave trade had annoyed the Sudanese, but the main inspiration was a religious one following the declaration of Muhammed Ahmed that he was the Mahdi—the Expected Deliverer of Islam.

Baring, who had assumed control of Egyptian affairs at the beginning of 1883, advised the Gladstone government that the only sensible course was for Egypt to withdraw. Gladstone had already concluded that Britain had taken on enough responsibility in Egypt, and he believed that the Sudanese were 'struggling rightly to be free' from Egyptian misgovernment. However, Gladstone was willing to admit that Britain had a duty to withdraw the Egyptian garrisons in the Sudan before they were annihilated. Gladstone's decision to 'rescue and retire' provoked a vote of censure in the House of Commons, which was only narrowly rejected. The Liberal government sent General Charles Gordon to the Sudan in 1884.

'Chinese' Gordon was the last man to lead a retreat, especially from a country of which he had once been governor. He had won fame in China and was already a public hero before he became governor of the Sudan in 1874. There he had attempted to destroy the slave trade by a combination of Bible-reading and force of arms. At the beginning of January 1884 Gordon had already declared in the *Pall Mall Gazette* that the Mahdi could be effectively resisted. Gladstone and Baring had serious doubts about his appointment, but it seems likely that Granville saw in Gordon a popular hero who would make it less obvious to public opinion that there was to be a retreat. Gladstone merely wished Gordon to report on the position in the Sudan, to advise rather than act. Baring, however, wished for someone with executive power to organise the evacuation as quickly as possible. It was Granville, Hartington, Dilke and Northbrook who gave Gordon his orders at the War Office. The official written instructions stressed his advisory capacity, but at the same time indicated that he would receive further instructions from Baring. It is clear, however, from Gordon's own correspondence that he believed it was intended he should organise the evacuation of Egyptian troops from the Sudan. Confusion had set in from the moment of Gordon's appointment, and remained throughout the whole episode.

Once installed in Khartoum, the capital of the Sudan, Gordon ignored his instructions to evacuate, and by the end of March 1884 Khartoum was besieged by the Mahdi. Gladstone and Granville preferred to leave Gordon to his fate once he had defied orders, but Hartington, Dilke and Chamberlain pressed for assistance to be sent. The Cabinet reached a decision to send help on 12th February, but this help did not leave England until the end of October. The Cabinet, despite the worsening situation at Khartoum, argued through the spring and summer about the size and scope of the relief expedition, and whether a minister was to be sent with it. When Lord Wolseley's relief expedition reached Khartoum on 28th January 1885, they were two days late. Gordon was dead. The British government now abandoned the Sudan to the Mahdi, despite Egyptian protests.

Gladstone the G.O.M.—Grand Old Man—overnight became the M.O.G.—murderer of Gordon. The government was clearly at fault. The rebellion in the Sudan had not threatened British interests in Egypt, and though the muddle of Gordon's orders involved Gordon and Baring as well as Granville, Hartington, Northbrook and Dilke, once the danger to Gordon was known prompt action should have been the order of the day. It is difficult not to agree with Baring that 'the Nile expedition was sanctioned too late, and the reason why it was sanctioned too late was that Mr. Gladstone would not accept simple evidence of a plain fact which was patent to much less powerful intellects than his own'.

The affair had no great effect in diplomatic circles, except perhaps to encourage Russia in Afghanistan. Its importance lies in its revelation of Gladstone's dilemma when faced with the need for actions of which he did not basically approve. Its real impact was felt at home. The Queen's declaration that 'Mr. Gladstone and the government have Gordon's innocent, noble, heroic blood on their consciences' was a reflection of a large section of contemporary opinion. Seton-Watson has asserted that 'nothing—not even the Home Rule dispute—did so much to discredit the Liberal government with the nation at large, and to kindle those bitter feelings which were soon to split the Liberal party'.

Britain's concern both for the route to India and her immediate financial interests seems to have played a part in the decisions to occupy Egypt and not to occupy the Sudan. This concern also dictated policy in Southern Africa, where the danger came less from the intervention of other European powers and more from internal difficulties—the warlike Zulus and, as Robinson and Gallagher have emphasised, the awakening racial solidarity of the Boers, who were faced with the new imperial aggression of Britain dictated by the expansion of British business interests.

With the Sand River Convention óf 1852 and the Convention of Bloemfontein in 1854, Britain had abandoned her attempts to maintain sovereignty over the Boers, who had trekked northwards from Cape Colony, and the Conventions recognised respectively the independence of the Transvaal Republic and the Orange Free State. Cape Colony and the Natal seemed a sufficient base from which to secure the Cape route to India. Ideas of a federal union were rumoured, but never acted upon.

Improving relations with the Boers were shattered, however, by two rather high-handed actions of Gladstone's first government. First in 1868 Britain proclaimed a protectorate over Basutoland, bordering the Orange Free State on the south. The government claimed it was acting in the interests of peace by attempting to prevent the Basuto peoples from raiding the Free State for cattle. To the Boers it appeared as a policy intended to prevent their annexation of Basutoland. They were further angered in 1871 when Britain annexed Griqualand West, which bordered the Orange Free State on the west. The British government claimed that the discovery of a diamond field in the area necessitated the enforcement of law and order to protect British subjects. They were also anxious to protect the beginnings of investment and railway-building in the area. Even though the matter was solved by arbitration, a Gladstonian gesture, the Boers again accused the British of forestalling their own annexation.

For Lord Carnarvon, Disraeli's Colonial Secretary, who had sponsored the Federation of Canada Act in 1867, the aim was the

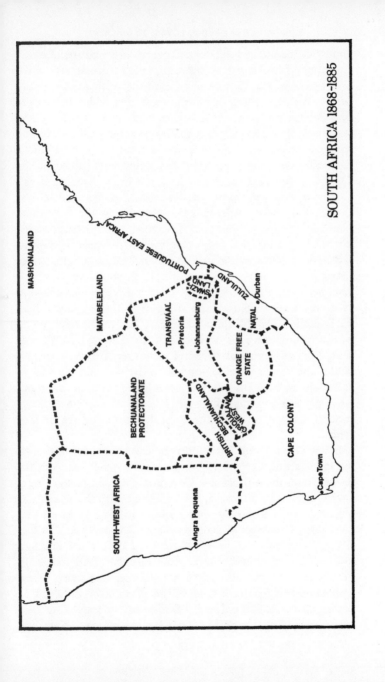

SOUTH AFRICA 1868-1885

MASHONALAND

MATABELELAND

PORTUGUESE EAST AFRICA

BECHUANALAND
PROTECTORATE

TRANSVAAL

•Pretoria

•Johannesburg

SWAZI-
LAND

ZULULAND

•Durban

NATAL

ORANGE FREE
STATE

BRITISH
BECHUANALAND

STELLALAND
GRIQUA
WEST

CAPE COLONY

SOUTH-WEST AFRICA

•Angra Pequena

•Cape Town

same, but the method different. Carnarvon revived the idea of a federation of South Africa, although, unlike Canada, few of the colonists wanted it. Carnarvon believed that such a union would both be a check on the Boers and would give added strength to deal with the problems of the warlike Bantu and the wild mining communities. Although lacking government approval colonisation had gone so far that there was now nothing for it but to bring the dependencies and the republics together in confederation. The Boer republics were not in a mood to co-operate, but Carnarvon believed that if the Transvaal, to the north of the Orange Free State, were annexed, both it and the Free State would be more amenable to federation. Carnarvon decided to send Sir Theophilus Shepstone, the ex-Lieutenant-Governor of Natal, to Pretoria, the capital of the Transvaal, with secret instructions to annex the republic, if circumstances made it possible. Shepstone found the Transvaal virtually bankrupt, with only twelve shillings and sixpence in the treasury, whilst the intensification of Zulu pressure gave him the justification he needed for annexing the territory in 1877. The republic's president, Burgers, who had talked of calling on Germany, agreed to the annexation provided he was pensioned and allowed to protest in public. Disraeli was not pleased with the position, especially as it brought Britain face to face with the Zulus. However, the annexation seemed to boost the prestige of the government.

It was Disraeli's misfortune that he had to deal not only with the imperialistic Shepstone, but also at the same time with Sir Bartle Frere, the expansionist Governor of Cape Colony. Frere, having inherited a Transvaal border dispute with the Zulus, was prepared to hand over disputed territory to them provided that their ruler, Cetewayo, disbanded his army and received a British resident—an emasculation to which Frere knew the Zulu chief would refuse to submit. The Cabinet agreed to send troops on Frere's request, but also urged him to keep the peace. Frere ignored instructions and ordered the invasion of Zululand in January 1879. At Isandhlwana a British force attempted to hold off a surprise Zulu attack, but it was finally massacred. Natal was now threatened, but in spite of the disaster at Isandhlwana, the Zulus were defeated at Ulundi, Cetewayo was deposed and the Zulus' military power broken up. In Britain, however, it was the loss of lives and the expense of victory that assumed importance. Hicks Beach, the new Colonial Secretary, and the Queen defended Frere's actions, but Disraeli strongly disapproved. Disraeli, however, was forced to defend Frere against Gladstone's charge of wanton aggression, for though Disraeli had not countenanced Frere's plan, he was held responsible. With troops fighting in Afghanistan and South Africa, and with the height of the depression at home, 1879 was a bad year for Conservatism.

The power of the Zulus was broken, but the problem of the Transvaal remained. Initial resistance to annexation had been lessened by Frere's promise of self-government, and in denouncing Conservative policy in Southern Africa Gladstone had declared his sympathy for the right of small nations to rule themselves. Gladstone promised to abandon the Transvaal, but once in office he became preoccupied with his rôle of Chancellor of the Exchequer rather than Prime Minister. With the Zulus no longer a threat the Boers rebelled, defeated a British force at Majuba Hill in 1881, and themselves threatened Natal. The news revived the jingo sentiment which Gladstone was attempting to exorcise, and he now conceded from weakness what he had intended earlier to concede from strength. With the Convention of Pretoria Gladstone gave the Transvaal independence 'subject to the suzerainty of Her Majesty', which allowed Britain to control foreign policy and protected British property and business rights. When the Boers complained about the suzerainty clause the London Convention of 1884 omitted it, but kept the restrictions.

The Boers received the impression that they could do with the British what they pleased, and that delusion was an important contributory cause of the Boer War in 1899, a war that Gladstone had hoped to avert. The Pretoria and London conventions appeared to be a craven surrender of imperial interests, yet despite concessions to the Boers, the government had preserved its control over foreign policy and British property and business interests. Furthermore, in 1884 the government annexed Stella-land and Goshen, two small farmer republics set up by the Boers in 1882, and made them the Crown Colony of Bechuanaland. Gladstone declared that his intention was to preserve African and missionary interests in the area, especially their route to the north, but it was no mere accident that the annexation followed the proclamation in 1884 of a German colony in South West Africa, bordering the republics and posing a possible threat to the Cape. Furthermore the conflict between Boer and Britain was intensified by the discovery of gold in the Transvaal in 1886—the Boers were flooded with new immigrants, and British and colonial capitalists moved in. Britain's original concern for the Cape route to the East was leading her deeper into Africa. This was to involve not only the Boer War, in a final effort to capture the Transvaal, but also the pursuit of a policy that extended British authority from the Limpopo River to the Great Lakes in the north.

Chapter V

Gladstone and Ireland 1867-93

1 The Irish problem Writing of the situation in Ireland in 1815 E. L. Woodward summarises the Irish problem as essentially 'the problem of a standard of life'. This was still true of Ireland in 1867. There were some Irish Catholic freeholders who enjoyed a reasonable standard of existence, and some owned considerable estates; there were even tenant farmers who lived prosperously. Most people in Ireland, however, lived near starvation level, and though generalisations often give a false impression, the abject state of most Irish peasants is fully endorsed by the commissions and select enquiries, well over a hundred of them before 1870, which examined the difficulties of Ireland. Even after mass emigration abysmal conditions persisted, aggravated by a high birth-rate, which was not absorbed by an increase in the amount of land under cultivation. Nor did Ireland share in the immense development of British industry during the nineteenth century, which could have helped in the absorption of surplus labour. Only Belfast towards the end of the century went through a process of large-scale industrialisation.

The problem, however, was not simply one of underdevelopment. The whole issue was complicated by the difficulties of tenure. The Irish labourer supplemented his money wage, which was very low, by cultivating a plot of land for which he paid rent either in labour or, as the century progressed, with money. Such tenure made the labourer extremely vulnerable to bad harvests, and with the increase in population the value of his labour and the size of his plot of land gradually became smaller. Except in the northern provinces of Ulster, where the custom known as Ulster Tenant Right gave to the peasant due recognition of any unexhausted improvements if he left his farm, as well as some security of tenure, the Irish tenant had no rights. Writing in 1870 about the Irish tenant, J. S. Mill declared, 'If he were industrious or prudent, nobody but his landlord would gain; if he is lazy and intemperate, it is at his landlord's expense. A situation more devoid of motives to either labour or self-command, imagination itself cannot conceive. The inducements of a free being are taken away, and those of a slave not substituted.' Until the very end of the century, when 'Bloody' Balfour was Chief Secretary for Ireland and some real assistance was given to enable the tenant to buy his land, there was little to encourage experiments in the better utilisation of land.

P. S. O'Hegarty, in his history of Ireland, has summarised the degrading system of land tenure as it existed in most of Ireland before the passing of the 1870 Land Act: 'The Irish landlord let land, and land only, that is to say the naked unadorned soil. The tenant who put up a fence, drained a boggy patch, whitewashed his house, put in a window or had a decent suit of clothes, had his rent increased; on very many estates no tenant was allowed to keep a friend or a relative in his house for even one night, he could not marry his son or daughter without permission, if he had a large holding he could not put up a house without permission. Practically every relation in his life was subject to arbitrary control, and if he offended against any of the rules of the particular estate on which he lived, he was subject to immediate eviction. And eviction meant starvation, beggary or emigration.' O'Hegarty is, of course, a patriot, but his view of the land system as a combination of feudalism and twentieth-century apartheid contains the unpleasant truth about many Irish estates.

Before Gladstone's first administration little was done to improve the situation in Ireland. This would seem to be due largely to the fact that the landlord in Ireland was both Protestant and of English extraction. Redress of Ireland's grievances could only be obtained from the Westminster Parliament, and that was the bastion of English landlord vested interests. State intervention would be an invasion of property rights in Ireland, and would open the way (as it did) to the invasion of property rights in England. The Irish problem was a distinct problem, but politically Ireland was not a separate unit, and landlord vested interests strongly opposed separate treatment for Ireland. Thus it is possible to agree with the conclusion reached by Nicholas Mansergh in his survey, *The Irish Question*: 'The fear of the possible repercussions of action in Ireland on society and interests in England was an all-important consideration, which would of necessity have applied, irrespective of the doctrines of economists, so long as opinion in Parliament was resolutely opposed to intervention by the state in principle and so long as the great majority of its members were men of substantial property.'

In addition it would seem that the need for reform in Ireland was shrouded in ignorance. Despite the vast accumulation of official reports few British statesmen, not even those like Lord Palmerston who were Irish landlords, had any first-hand knowledge of Irish conditions, and, therefore, lacked a sense of urgency concerning the settlement of the Irish problem. Gladstone visited Ireland once briefly in 1877, and Disraeli never at all. Official reports, it would seem, however numerous or well-documented, were no substitute for personal experience. For this reason it has been argued that men who lived otherwise virtuous and respectable lives inadvertently condoned the miseries of the Irish. Ignorance does not seem a convincing explanation for the reluctance to reform Ireland, especially as those who failed to sympathise with the Irish found it quite easy to sympathise with Italians and Balkan Christians about whom they knew even less. It was not lack of knowledge which delayed reform in Ireland, but the distorted view of Ireland occasioned by English religious and nationalist prejudices. It was these prejudices that were marshalled for the attack on Gladstone's policy of reform. As Home Rule replaced land reform as the demand of the Irish, the economic problem of Irish land tenures was replaced by the need to find some political solution for the Irish. Gladstone found that the Irish problem by the late nineteenth century was not simply a matter of economic reform. There were further, acute complications.

Although O'Connell had at length secured equal legal status for Catholics, the English dislike and fear of Catholicism had a long history which no Act of Parliament could abolish. Ireland remained in the nineteenth century a centre of potential rebellion and possible treason, and hence the weak point of Great Britain's defensive strategy. It was essentially for this reason that the Catholic Irish majority found themselves ruled over by a Protestant minority, which was supported by the British government. Religious prejudice was the easiest way to raise a popular wall of no-surrender to Irish demands, and was used unscrupulously by the opponents of Irish nationalist rights, not least by Lord Randolph Churchill. The fear of popery also helped to split the Liberal Nonconformist ranks, caught between their moral political philosophy and hatred of the anti-Christ of Rome. Far too many Englishmen were convinced that Home Rule would lead to Rome rule. Religious antagonism seems to explain why the Irish problem aroused popular passions, but it does not fully explain why many distinguished statesmen in the Westminster Parliament, and especially in the Liberal party, opposed Ireland's demand for self-government.

By the end of the nineteenth century the Irish problem was increasingly becoming an issue of nationalism, and involved itself in that wider nationalism—the Empire. There was a genuine dilemma. In a democracy the majority is held to be right. In the United Kingdom in the nineteenth century the majority were opposed to the Irish demand to rule themselves, but in Ireland a majority wanted political independence of some sort. The Irish problem by the late nineteenth century had become the insurmountable question of which majority was to be respected. The fact that the United Kingdom was the centre of a vast Empire added further complications. Nationalism in Europe might be encouraged if it suited Britain's interests, but nationalism within the British Empire was to be put down with the same force, and often the same means, as the Austrians used against the

Italians. To many Home Rule for Ireland was simply the tip of a separatist iceberg, and the Irish were no better than those Boers, Indians or Egyptians who sought the disruption of the Empire. Gladstone's Home Rule Bills were defeated by a combination of religious prejudice, nationalist passion and imperial pride.

When in 1868 Gladstone turned away from the trees he was felling to hear that he was to become Prime Minister for the first time, he declared, 'My mission is to pacify Ireland.' He thus embarked on his greatest and most frustrating crusade. The Irish problem defeated him. By 1885 Gladstone was one of the few statesmen who appreciated that the Irish problem was a combination of economic, religious and nationalist factors. Such an appreciation, however, did not guarantee success. It was one thing to understand the Irish problem, but another to solve it.

2 **Pacification** The question 'Why did Gladstone become so sympathetically involved with Ireland?' is an obvious one to ask, but considering the difficulties and misfortunes that resulted, perhaps a more pertinent question would be, 'Why did Gladstone remain involved for so long?'

Gladstone had shown an early interest in Ireland, and in 1841 he had hoped in vain for the Chief Secretaryship of Ireland in Peel's government. His motive, however, appears to have been a desire to follow in the footsteps of Peel rather than a youthful wish to solve the Irish problem. It was Gladstone's interest in Italy that first produced a sympathetic approach to Ireland, and as J. L. Hammond has remarked, 'Gladstone found in the nationalist spirit in revolt in Ireland something akin to the spirit that had drawn his sympathy to the Italian movement.' When Russell had despatched his famous telegram to Hudson in Turin in 1860, Gladstone was deeply affected by the Austrian reply, which compared their actions in Italy with Britain's actions in Ireland. Gladstone thus became aware that there was an Irish problem, and the Fenian outrages of 1865-7 shocked him into activity.

The Irish Republican Brotherhood, later known as the Fenian Brotherhood, was founded in the United States; its aim was to establish by any means an Irish Republic. The development of the Brotherhood in Ireland was delayed by the American Civil War, but after 1865 it spread rapidly. The acts of terror carried out by the Fenians won little sympathy from the British government, which replied with Coercion Bills, and finally by the suspension of Habeas Corpus. The Fenians, however, never gained a real hold on the Irish peasantry, who in the struggle for survival lacked the time and the energy for prolonged rebellion. This failure of the Fenians convinced Gladstone of two things: that the redress of agrarian grievances and the abolition of the privileges of the Anglican Church in Ireland would help to bring about a long-delayed reconciliation, and that delay was dangerous, for next time the Fenians might succeed. It was in this spirit that he embarked on his policy of pacification. Once launched on his crusade Gladstone became more involved as his understanding of the Irish problem increased.

Gladstone's concern for Ireland was not a freak part of his career; it was very much an essential aspect of his thinking, developing as his liberal philosophy matured. Gladstonian Liberalism was an Irish as well as an English phenomenon. Gladstone believed that all men had certain inalienable rights merely by virtue of their humanity, and by 1868 he was convinced that these rights had been refused to Irishmen. As his Liberalism progressed, as his sympathy with the nationalist movements in Europe deepened, Gladstone became convinced that these inalienable rights had been denied the Irish not merely as men, but as a nation as well. This development marks his shift from mere pacification to Home Rule for Ireland.

Gladstone's resolution in the House of Commons that the Irish Church 'as a state church must cease to exist' brought down Disraeli's first ministry in 1868, and became the issue in the election of that year. Gladstone was on fairly safe ground, for except in South-West Lancashire, his own seat, he captured the vote of the Nonconformists who were glad to weaken the Anglican Church. He took the precaution of standing also for Greenwich, where he was returned with a comfortable majority. The new government proceeded almost immediately with the Disestablishment Act of 1869, which confiscated all the property, mainly land and tithe rent charge, of the Established Church in Ireland. The confiscated property was then used for a variety of public purposes and to endow the Irish Anglican Church as a new self-governing and self-financing corporation. The Bill was carried easily in the Commons, and, despite many anxious moments, was accepted by the House of Lords. With a clear Liberal majority in the Commons of 112, elected under the new franchise, the Lords and the Queen were anxious to avoid anything that might upset the constituencies, and despite the efforts of Disraeli and his Ulster colleague, Lord Cairns, Lord Salisbury declared that where the electorate had spoken clearly, it was not the business of the Lords to resist the nation's will. This view was shared by Archbishop Tait of Canterbury, who led the Church party. They followed a policy of moderation in an effort to secure for the Irish Church the largest possible endowment.

The Act did not have a profound effect upon the Irish, for much of their active hatred for the Church had been transferred to the landlord, when tithes collection became the responsibility of the latter. In retrospect, however, the Act emerges as an important milestone, and it is possible to agree with O'Hegarty's assessment: 'It was the first breach of the Union, against the most determined opposition of those in Ireland who profited by the Union, and for those whose benefit it had been established and maintained.' Gladstone, as soon as the Act was passed, immersed himself for three months in the problems of Irish agriculture, for he realised that real improvement in Ireland would depend on success in this sphere.

The Irish Land Act passed in 1870 allowed loans of public money to tenants for the purchase of their holdings, limited the landlord's powers of arbitrary eviction, and enforced compensation for improvements even in cases of eviction for non-payment of rent. The custom of tenant right in Ulster, and similar usages elsewhere, were recognised in law. In addition a scale of damages was established for eviction, varying according to the size of the holding (the smaller the holding the higher the rate of compensation), though no payment for disturbance was made in cases of eviction due to a failure to pay rent. Only eleven members voted against the Bill's second reading in the House of Commons, whilst the House of Lords did not divide upon the second reading. Both parties agreed that something had to be done for the Irish tenants, and even the diehards in the Lords were not yet ready to challenge the Commons. But the Act was not a success.

The Act was not what the Irish tenants wanted. Their great wish was not to be compensated when they were evicted, but to be secure against eviction. Despite his three months of detailed study Gladstone had failed to grasp the situation in Ireland, ignoring the 'Three Fs' demanded by the Irish Tenant Right Party—free sale of the tenant's interest in the property; fair rent established by evaluation; fixity of tenure so long as a fair rent was paid. Gladstone, with the best intentions, had failed to look at tenure from an Irish point of view, and did not yet realise that Irish tenants thought of themselves as part owners of the land on which they worked. Gladstone's 'awakening' did not come until the depression after 1875 added further grief, violence and bitterness to the Irish problem. Even the Land Act of 1870 had to be followed in the next year by a Coercion Bill to stamp out agricultural crime in Ireland.

Since the approach to the problem was misconceived, it is not surprising to find faults in the provisions of the Act. What protection was offered by the Act was easily evaded. The original Bill had provided courts to revise *excessive* rents, but in the Lords the clause had been changed to *exorbitant* rents, and the courts themselves tended to dispense class justice by ruling in the interests of the landlord. Thus the revolution on paper was of little help in practice, especially when put to the test of the depression in agriculture in the late seventies. Landlords sought to protect themselves by raising rents, rents which tenants were expected to find from falling agricultural prices. The more ambitious landlords, who sought to reorganise their estates in order to survive, found it all too easy to raise rents so high as to force their tenants into arrears, so that they could evict them. The measure intended to protect the smaller tenant by offering him a higher rate of compensation served merely to encourage the landlord to get rid of him. Even the clauses which reflected

Bright's idea of encouraging tenants to purchase their holdings were a failure, for they were cumbersome and unattractive. One important consequence of the Act was to establish the principle that property in land was not absolute, but this was certainly not Gladstone's intention. He wished only to protect tenants from unfair treatment, and in this the 1870 Act failed.

Despite the weaknesses of the Land Act, Ireland entered a brief period of comparative calm before the storm broke with the coming of the depression. Gladstone's plans for pacification included also the setting up of a Royal Residence in Ireland, and establishing a vice-royalty as a ceremonial position for the Prince of Wales, whilst a minister would be appointed who would be a Secretary of State. But Queen Victoria would not agree to giving the Prince of Wales any duty of importance, and was not prepared to accept the idea of a Royal Residence, as she feared she might be expected to visit Ireland more often. Gladstone did persist, however, with his scheme to create an Irish university for both Protestants and Roman Catholics. His plan was to combine Trinity College Dublin, Maynooth and the colleges of Cork and Belfast into one university, which, by excluding theology, moral philosophy and history from the curriculum, Gladstone hoped would unite Protestants and Catholics. Unfortunately for Gladstone's hopes, many Catholics preferred a Catholic university, whilst many Protestants opposed the loss of Trinity College. The Irish University Bill of 1873 was defeated by three votes, with forty-three Liberals voting in the majority. The defeat of the Bill indicated clearly for the first time the danger to the Liberal party of too radical an espousal of the Irish cause. But the cause was not abandoned, and as soon as the Liberals were returned to office in 1880 a new Irish Land Bill was promoted.

The Bill of 1880 proposed to give tenants temporary security in their land tenure, even if they had not paid rent for three years. Though passed in the Commons, it was rejected by the Lords. Forster, now Chief Secretary for Ireland, warned the Lords that such abuse of their power would lead to its removal. Gladstone, who had been involved in foreign and financial affairs, had paid little attention to Ireland since becoming Prime

Minister, but the wave of violence and unrest that followed the rejection of the 1880 Bill, and the need for a Coercion Bill that suspended Habeas Corpus, forced Gladstone into new activity. A commission presided over by Lord Bessborough was set up to suggest revisions of the 1870 Act, and Gladstone accepted their far-reaching findings, which were embodied in the 1881 Irish Land Act. This revealed the great development of Gladstone's understanding of the Irish problem.

The new Land Act extended and legalised Ulster tenant rights throughout Ireland by giving the tenant greater security of tenure, and the right to sell his interest in his holding. At the same time judicial tribunals were established to fix fair rents for a period of fifteen years. The Irish had secured their 'Three Fs'. The agricultural problem was taken out of Anglo-Irish politics. William O'Brien, one of Parnell's associates, said of the Act: 'It raised the Irish tenant from a tenure more precarious than that of any peasantry in Europe to an acknowledged legal partnership with the landlord in the ownership of his fields; and it reduced the landlords from a power as unbridled as that of a Turkish pasha over his slaves, to the position of annuitants, entitled to what was decreed by a court of equity to be a fair rent, and to scarcely any other vestige of their former sovereign privileges.' The Act, though, did have its faults. Tenants in arrears with rent were not included, and the Act was still conceived in English terms of tenant farmers rather than peasant ownership. Loans were offered to enable tenants to buy their farms, though the provision was rather limited, and this part of the Act was little used. Yet the greatest flaw of the Act was its occasion rather than any of its provisions. Once again the government at Westminster conceded to violence and crime what it had denied to reason and justice. Parnell, the Irish leader, fully appreciated this fact, and organised his tactics around it.

Gladstone's part in Irish history cannot be denied, but though Disraeli in office did little to help Ireland, perhaps too aware of the dangers of a Conservative revolt on this issue, he is often credited with a real sympathy for the Irish cause. In a speech made in 1844 Disraeli summed up the Irish problem as 'a starving population, an absentee aristocracy, an alien Church, and in addition the weakest executive in the world'. Furthermore in both 1852 and 1855 when he was Chancellor of the Exchequer he made suggestions for Irish land reform. However, other evidence questions Disraeli's sympathy for Ireland. His maiden speech in the House of Commons, although usually remembered for its confusion and failure, was in fact an attack on O'Connell. A year ealier, in 1836, Disraeli had written in *The Times*, 'This wild, reckless, indolent, uncertain and superstitious race have no sympathy with the English character.' His proposals of 1852 and 1855 can too easily be interpreted as those of a minority government anxious to win friends in any quarter. After 1874, apart from concern over the obstructive tactics of the Irish party, Disraeli's government showed little interest in Ireland beyond some ineffective efforts to encourage education. It is possible to agree with Mansergh and others that Disraeli, like Gladstone, appreciated the European background to the Irish problem, but Disraeli's appreciation seems to have led him to a different conclusion from Gladstone's. Disraeli saw Ireland as Britain's parallel to the Balkans, and in both cases he preferred aristocratic rule to native independence. The feudal ideals of 'Young England' influenced Disraeli's attitude to peasant societies. The election of 1880 produced a last policy statement from Disraeli on Ireland. In his election address he warned the nation of the dangers of Home Rule. It was rather a damp squib, as there was no Unionist sentiment to be rallied to the defence of the Act of Union in 1880, when the Liberal party was officially as uncommitted to Home Rule as the Conservatives. Disraeli's manifesto was six years too soon. Buckle regarded the manifesto as evidence of Disraeli's foresight, but it can also be seen, as Blake has pointed out, as an attempt to distract public attention from the failures of the government by stirring up racial prejudice.

3 Gladstone, Parnell and Home Rule   The worst features of Irish agricultural distress gradually disappeared as the Land Act of 1881, and its successors, were implemented, but Ireland's demand for self-government, for Home Rule, continued. Pacification had removed the worst manifestations of English rule in Ireland, but not what now emerged as the root cause of Irish discontent—English rule itself. By 1885 Gladstone had become convinced that Home Rule ought to be granted. To understand how this 'conversion' came about it is necessary to examine the development of the Home Rule movement under Parnell's leadership, and Gladstone's reactions to it.

The Home Rule League had been founded in Dublin in 1870 under the leadership of Isaac Butt. Butt was a Protestant and a lawyer, who had defended a number of Fenians in court and convinced himself of the need to change Ireland's form of government. The Home Rule League was not opposed to the Union, but aimed to establish within the framework of the United Kingdom a subordinate legislature for Ireland, with power to pass laws for local Irish purposes. The Home Rulers, taking advantage of the extension of the franchise and the Ballot Act of 1872, the latter enabling tenants to vote without fear of their landlords, won sixty seats in the 1874 election, and sat on the opposition benches with the Liberals.

Butt believed separation would be disastrous, but not as disastrous as the continual misgovernment of Ireland by Westminster. He hoped that reform would lead to the abatement of the demand for Home Rule, but he supported Home Rule as the only solution to end the governing of Ireland perpetually against her will. Butt's approach, however, was that of the lawyer rather than the political agitator, for he had great respect for the traditions of the House of Commons. Others, notably Joseph Biggar, were less deferential. It was Biggar who embarked on a policy of obstruction at Westminster, and by keeping carefully to the rules of procedure, he was able to delay the business of the House of Commons by speaking at enormous length. Parnell adopted Biggar's tactics and refined them, organising a team of speakers and introducing amendments and motions for adjournment. The object of obstruction was to demonstrate that if the English members would not co-operate on Irish affairs, then the Irish members would make it difficult for them to deal with English affairs. Obstruction succeeded in little more than annoying the government. But the advent of Parnell transformed the Home Rule League into a popular nationalist movement.

Charles Stewart Parnell was a Protestant landowner, born in 1846, the son of an Anglo-Irish father and an American mother. It is common to attribute Parnell's hatred of England to his mother, even though she appears to have been a frequent and willing visitor to Dublin Castle. Parnell in fact seems to have been made more aware of his nationality by the arrogance of his English schoolfellows, and his education in England rather than his mother's influence may account for his attitudes. Parnell espoused the Irish cause early in his life, and the Ballot Act of 1872 inspired him to declare, 'Now something can be done if full advantage will be taken of this Ballot Act!' He entered Parliament in 1875, having failed in his first attempt the previous year, supported and then supplanted Biggar, and by 1877 was already convinced that 'we shall never gain anything from England unless we tread on her toes; we will never gain a single sixpennyworth from her by conciliation'. Butt objected to obstruction tactics, but Parnell pushed him aside (Butt died in 1879), and dominated the movement until his own fall. Yet despite the activities of the Home Rulers at Westminster, they were a small minority of Irish opinion, and it was the newly formed Irish Land League that appealed most to the Irish peasant. Parnell's great achievement was to unite the followers of both Leagues.

The Land League had been formed in 1879 by Michael Davitt. Davitt's Catholic family had been evicted from their land and had emigrated to Lancashire when he was five years old. There he had first lost an arm in a factory accident, and then become involved in the Fenian movement, and had eventually spent seven degrading years in Dartmoor Prison. Released from prison Davitt visited America, returning to Ireland at the height of the depression. By 1879 the situation for most Irish peasants was desperate. Competition from America drastically lowered agricultural prices, and rents which had been reasonable became exorbitant. Evictions followed. The short-term object of the Land League was to secure immediate relief by reducing rents; the long-term object was to end the problem by making the occupiers the owners of the soil. Parnell was not at first involved with the Land League, but in October 1879 he accepted the leadership of the movement, and at once his position was transformed. He was no longer simply the leader of a small group in the House of Commons playing games at Westminster, but also the leader of a growing popular movement on a national scale.

A tour of America secured £50,000 for the League to aid distress, but when the Lords rejected the Land Bill of 1880, the situation in Ireland rapidly deteriorated. The Land League advised tenants to give first consideration to their families before paying rent, and when a Captain Boycott evicted a tenant for non-payment of rent, Parnell urged that he and his like should be 'isolated from his kind as if he were a leper of old'—and a new word was added to the English language. An attempt to prosecute the leaders of the Land League for conspiracy failed when the jury could not reach agreement, and though Forster pushed through his Coercion Bill of 1881 in the face of an orgy of obstruction, Gladstone made sure that his second Land Act was secured also. It was in 1881 that Gladstone's conversion to Home Rule probably began.

What shocked Gladstone into a new awareness of the Irish problem was the refusal of the Irish party to abandon their aggressive tactics and co-operate over the implementation of the Land Act. Parnell insisted on maintaining the pressure on the English as the only way of securing future concessions. It was this continued activity which appears to have made Gladstone first aware of the limitations of his policy of pacification. Clearly agrarian reform would not secure reconciliation. The outrages continued, and Gladstone's first reaction was to agree to his colleagues' demands for the internment of Parnell in Kilmainham Gaol and the suppression of the Land League. Parnell thus became the first in a long line of nationalist leaders, including Gandhi, Nkrumah and Kenyatta, to be imprisoned by British governments which disapproved of their political tactics.

Gladstone, however, was not convinced that suppression and coercion were the answer—they had not worked in the past. He was not pleased with his surrender to Forster and the Whig landlords in the Cabinet, and in April 1882 he reached an understanding with Parnell—the Kilmainham 'Treaty'. There was in fact no treaty, but Gladstone agreed to an Arrears Bill by which 100,000 Irish tenants who owed large arrears of rent, and therefore could not make use of the Land Act, would be freed from debt. In return Parnell and his colleagues promised to use their influence to bring about peace in Ireland. Parnell was released, but Lord Cowper the Viceroy, and Forster the Chief Secretary, resigned in protest. The Kilmainham 'Treaty' did not recognise Parnell as the leader of an independent nation, but it was an admission by Gladstone that English government in Ireland could not secure a peaceable return to order, and it was a recognition of the fact that only the leaders of the Irish could achieve government by the consent of the people. Home Rule was a real possibility.

A new and happier period in Irish affairs, however, was forestalled when the new Viceroy, Lord Frederick Cavendish, a member of Gladstone's own family circle, and the Undersecretary Burke, were hacked to death with long surgical knives in Phoenix Park, Dublin in May 1882, four days after Parnell's release. The assassins were later identified as a small murder club known as the 'Invincibles'. Parnell and Gladstone made a real attempt to save the Kilmainham alliance. From the moment Parnell accepted the Land Act, Gladstone no longer treated him as a public enemy, and became increasingly willing to work with him. However, a new and stiffer Coercion Bill was inevitable, and Parnell opposed it. Apart from declaring boycotting illegal, the Act replaced trial by jury with trial by judges, and secret enquiries were permitted. At the same time an Act was passed permitting closure of debate, enabling the Speaker of the House of Commons to end debates and thus avoid obstructionist tactics. Although obstruction continued it had less effect and ceased to be the main tactic of the Irish party. Despite the breakdown in relations, Gladstone insisted on an Arrears Bill being passed, though it was not generous enough for most tenants to be able to use it.

1882 appears as a year of lost opportunity. O'Hegarty has argued that the murders postponed Home Rule until Conservative opinion had hardened into opposition, and that in 1882 Gladstone with a large majority was sympathetically inclined towards Home Rule. There would probably have been only a minor Home Rule Act, but it would have established a principle that could have been widened. There is, however, only a suspicion and not evidence of Gladstone's sympathy for Home Rule, and it is difficult to imagine anything but Conservative opposition to any suggestion of Home Rule, however limited. The assassinations were a disaster because they confirmed English public opinion in its belief that the Irish were irresponsible and violent, and made the Irish task of persuading politicians and public to accept Home Rule immeasurably more difficult.

By the end of 1883 Irish affairs had grown quieter as the Land Act began to take effect. Gladstone became increasingly involved in the problems of Egypt and a new Reform Bill. Parnell, however, was planning for the next round. The Irish National League in 1882 replaced the Land League as Parnell's popular organisation. The pressure in the agrarian sphere had been reduced, and Parnell was now anxious to organise a victory for Home Rule. His plan was not to obstruct the workings of the English Parliament, but instead to bargain with one of the English parties. By securing the Irish party's control over what turned out to be eighty-five seats in Ireland and one in Liverpool, Parnell hoped to prove a valuable asset in the forming of a British government, and this fact was not ignored by the more unscrupulous politicians in both parties. The use that could be made of the Irish members was demonstrated on 9th June 1885, when Gladstone's second administration was brought down by a combination of Conservatives and Irish organised by Parnell and Lord Randolph Churchill. Lord Salisbury's 'caretaker' government was dependent on the Irish vote, and Salisbury went out of his way to retain the goodwill of Parnell. The result was the end of Lord Spencer's strong government in Ireland, and the first state-assisted land purchase scheme for Ireland—Ashbourne's Act, 1885—sponsored by a Conservative government. Many were astounded at the reversal of Conservative policy, but no one was quite as explicit as Joseph Chamberlain, who denounced the whole manoeuvre as 'astounding tergiversation . . . the most flagrant instance of political dishonesty this country has ever known'.

Parnell was delighted. Even before the election of 1885, Churchill from the Conservatives and Chamberlain from the Liberals were anxious to have dealings with him. Parnell did not mind from what party he obtained Home Rule, as long as it was obtained. He believed, however, that only the Conservatives could secure an easy passage of a Home Rule Bill through the House of Lords, and Lord Carnarvon, Salisbury's Viceroy, seemed prepared to make concessions towards self-government. At the same time the discreet silence of Salisbury and Churchill encouraged Parnell to believe that the Conservatives would co-operate. Two days before the 1885 election Parnell issued a manifesto instructing the Irish throughout the United Kingdom to vote against all Liberal and Radical candidates. In the election Parnell's party secured a bloc of eighty-six seats, the Liberals secured 335 seats and the Conservatives 249. Parnell was in a position to keep either party out of office, but he could only put the Liberals in. This had disastrous effects, not least that Salisbury returned to a policy of coercion.

Parnell's leadership of the Home Rule movement had secured its greatest coup in 1885—both the English parties were seduced by his success. It was a quirk of fate that the figures in the election were as they were; Parnell had stopped a Liberal landslide victory, and they too were now to seek an Irish alliance. But Home Rule for Ireland was not a foregone conclusion.

Gladstone's position during the summer of 1885 is difficult to disentangle, not least because he was deliberately obscure. Morley's description of Gladstone at this time is: 'A pilot amid wandering icebergs, or in waters where familiar buoys had been taken up and immemorial beacons put out, he scanned the scene with keen eyes and a glass sweeping the horizon in every direction.' Gladstone, however, may well have had a more definite policy than Morley was aware of. Magnus has argued that Gladstone finally made up his mind to support Home Rule when on holiday in Norway in 1885, that Gladstone found in Norway a small people living happily in a spirit of democracy under the sovereignty of Sweden, and that the effect upon his mind was comparable with that of his visit ·ɔ Naples in the winter of 1850. The visit to Norway may have produced the final crystallisation, but Lord Randolph Churchill pointed out in the debates that followed that Gladstone had never spoken against Home Rule since 1881. Gladstone may have been motivated by moral considerations suddenly to support Home Rule, but there is much evidence also to indicate that he was a clever and practical politician. There were good reasons why Gladstone should not reveal his conversion to Home Rule before he was forced to it. Gladstone was opposed to bidding for the Irish vote, for the Conservatives could offer passage through the House of Lords and might win the vote instead. He was also aware of the danger of arousing uncompromising Conservative opposition to all proposals for Irish self-government. Further, he did not want to risk a division in the Liberal party before an election. Primarily however, Gladstone seems to have believed, like Parnell, that the only sure way of securing Home Rule was for a Conservative government to carry it with Liberal and Irish support. Thus Mansergh has concluded, 'Influenced by the precedents of Catholic Emancipation (1829), of the Repeal of the Corn Laws (1846), and the Second Reform Bill (1867), Gladstone considered that the repeal of the Union could most surely be carried by a Conservative government, supported by Liberal votes to counterbalance the defection of the extreme Tories.' Gladstone was participating in a political manoeuvre rather than awaiting a volcanic eruption of his conscience.

The result of the 1885 election undermined Gladstone's 'plan', but he did not abandon it; he kept silent even when Parnell made overtures to the Liberal party. Gladstone hoped that Salisbury would still take the initiative, and for this purpose on 15th December he visited Arthur Balfour, Salisbury's Chief Secretary in Ireland, to persuade him of the need to grant Home Rule immediately. Whatever slight chance Gladstone had of encouraging the Conservatives was lost the next day, when his son Herbert informed the press of his father's conversion to Home Rule. The consequences of this Hawarden Kite were spectacular. Salisbury at once abandoned contact with Parnell, whilst in the Liberal camp Hartington warned Gladstone that he could not accept Home Rule. Chamberlain at first could not believe the news, but grew more irritable as the consequences dawned on him. Gladstone saw his schemes vanish overnight, and prepared instead to convert the country and his party to the policy of Home Rule for Ireland. The most dramatic party conflict of the century was about to begin. Gladstone had wanted a non-party effort to solve the Irish question, so that the settlement would be British, rather than Liberal or Conservative. Civil war in Ireland, which had seemed the worst of evils since 1828, now seemed to many statesmen a lesser evil than Home Rule. The crisis of 1885-6 created a combination of parties, not to obtain Home Rule, but to defeat it.

Gladstone has been heavily criticised for not informing others of his intentions, but the whole point of his reticence and secrecy was to allow the Conservatives to act so as to avoid party conflict, not least within the Liberal party. Even so, Gladstone's tactics of 1885 carried with them their unfortunate consequences when in January 1886 he assumed office again. His apparently sudden conversion threw into opposition men who otherwise might have been conciliated. Of his old colleagues, Hartington, Bright, Selborne and James refused to join the Cabinet, and Chamberlain resigned within two months. Morley gravely accepted the post of Chief Secretary, though Thomas Huxley warned him, 'He is sending you, my dear friend, to Ireland, as he sent Gordon to Khartoum.'

Nevertheless the Liberals who remained fought courageously for Home Rule, and the struggle became one of the most memorable in the annals of English parliamentary history. As Harcourt warned the opponents of the Home Rule Bill, 'You may reject this Bill, but its record will remain. The history of England and Ireland can never be as if this offer had never been made. You may kill it now, but its ghost will ever haunt your festivals of coercion '

In April 1886 Gladstone's Home Rule Bill was introduced. Chamberlain and Charles Trevelyan had already resigned, having seen the Bill in Cabinet. The Bill proposed to set up an Irish parliament and executive in Dublin which would have powers of legislation and control over all but reserved subjects such as peace and war, defence, foreign relations, customs and excise. Ireland was to provide one-fifteenth of the charges of the United Kingdom budget for 'imperial' purposes, mainly debt interest and defence, whilst the rest of the revenue raised there was at their own disposal. To safeguard the Protestant minority the Dublin parliament was to consist of two orders rather like a chamber and a senate, the latter to include twenty-eight elective Irish peers, but the two orders would sit together. Irish representatives were no longer to be present at Westminster unless summoned for the special task of reviewing the Home Rule Act. Irish judges were to be appointed by the Irish government, though with full right of appeal from the Irish courts to the Judicial Committee of the Privy Council in London. Gladstone accompanied the Home Rule Bill with a sweeping Land Purchase Bill, which planned to buy out landlords at approximately twenty years' purchase of their rentals.

Of all the details of Gladstone's Bill, the one most criticised was the exclusion of the Irish members from Westminster. It was argued that Ireland could never be held long under a British parliament which could fix taxes and pocket about forty per cent of the proceeds, but in which Ireland would be unrepresented. Many critics on the Conservative side, led by Lord Randolph Churchill, affected to be concerned for the Ulster Protestants. The Bill, however, was defeated not by the official opposition but by the Liberal renegades. On 8th June 1886 the second reading of the Bill was defeated by 343 votes to 313, ninety-three Liberals voting in the majority, and in the ensuing general election the Liberal-Irish alliance was defeated by 118 seats. Gladstone faced the bitterness of defeat once again. 'In his first two terms of office as Prime Minister', Hammond has remarked, 'he had spent on Ireland strength, health, power and popularity, as no politician had ever done.' In opposition he was to keep the Irish problem alive, despite the reluctance of his audiences to accept the justice of his arguments. Gladstone's courage can be admired, but can his wisdom? Why did Gladstone support Home Rule?

Gladstone's critics, beginning with Chamberlain, saw his support of Home Rule as an effort to secure the Irish vote in England and Scotland, which in turn would enable him to resist the pressure for radical reform growing within the rank and file of the Liberal party. Certainly Gladstone did not approve of Chamberlain's 'unauthorised programme', but if he had wanted to bid for the Irish vote, it is odd that he did not do so in the 1885 election. Furthermore, in the 1892 election Gladstone accepted the radicalism of the Newcastle programme, and the possibility of winning votes in this way to assist Home Rule. The most probable explanation for Gladstone's enthusiasm for the Irish cause remains that given by Hammond in *Gladstone and the Irish Nation*. Gladstone was convinced that Irish nationalism was not a passing mood but an inextinguishable passion, and that the safety as well as the credit of the British Empire depended on Britain's ability to solve the Irish problem. Gladstone wanted to see Ireland a free, vigorous society, and for that it was necessary to end the tradition of violence. At some time during or after 1881 Gladstone had been converted to the idea that Ireland needed her own social and political institutions, in the development of which she would engender self-respect and turn away from lawlessness. It was Gladstone's ability to place Ireland in a European context, to see Irish nationalism as part of the rising tide of European nationalism, which, Hammond has revealingly argued, placed Gladstone apart from many of his contemporaries, who saw Irish demands for self-government as an attempt to disrupt the British Empire. Gladstone's sympathy for nationalist movements, for their combined demand for self-determination and self-government, 'enabled him to divine the strength and the power of this passion in politics, and to know that Great Britain could not expect that there should be one law in history for Europe and another for the British Empire'. It was this understanding that enabled Gladstone to move from the pacification of religious and agrarian grievances to the gratification of the Irish demands for Ireland.

Gladstone was not alone in his miscalculations of developments in 1885-6; Parnell had made his mistakes. Parnell's election manifesto had turned into a terrible blunder, for though he had secured eighty-six seats for his own party, it is probable that he handed between twenty and forty seats to the Conservatives, and twenty-five votes could have reversed the decision of the House of Commons on the first Home Rule Bill. In the long term, the effect of Parnell's decision was even more disastrous. Parnell had tried to form what he called 'an independent opposition', which would be able to ally itself with whatever English party came nearest to Irish demands. After 1886 this policy of independence, except on minor issues, was no longer possible, for Home Rule could only be obtained from the Liberals. Thus the Liberal alliance became essential to the Irish parliamentary party, and the Liberals were to demand a high price for continuing this alliance when the O'Shea divorce scandal broke.

Parnell kept clear of the Plan of Campaign set up by John Dillon and William O'Brien following the renewal of agrarian distress, and was not involved in the Michelstown riot of 1887 when the police opened fire on the crowd which had collected there for the trial of O'Brien. A special commission set up by Salisbury's government also cleared Parnell of any implication in the Phoenix Park murders, and he began proceedings against *The Times* which had published a letter claiming he condoned the murders. There was even a reaction of public opinion in Parnell's favour. At the end of 1889, however, Captain O'Shea, one of Parnell's associates, petitioned for divorce alleging Parnell's adultery with Mrs. O'Shea. The suit was not contested.

Parnell claimed that his private life had nothing to do with his political work, and the League seemed to accept this view, and re-elected him leader in 1890. Unfortunately Gladstone declared unexpectedly, in a letter which Harcourt and Morley encouraged him to publish, that Parnell's leadership of the Irish party 'would render my retention of the leadership of the Liberal party, based as it has been mainly upon the prosecution of the Irish cause, almost a nullity'. This incident is often cited as an example of Gladstone's priggishness, but it seems more likely to have been an example of Gladstone's sense of political realities. The pressure on him came, not from his own conscience, but from the National Liberal Federation. Middle-class Nonconformity had been an essential ally of the Liberal party, which Gladstone had always taken pains to nourish. Gladstone, Harcourt and Morley forced the Irish party to renounce their leader not because they were shocked by his adulterous relationship with Mrs. O'Shea, of which they had known for at least seven years, but because of the thunderings of the Rev. Hugh Price Hughes, who denounced Parnell at the 1890 session of the National Liberal Federation. Ireland had already lost the Liberals the support of many Whigs and radicals, and Gladstone could not afford to lose the Nonconformist vote. His letter was deplorable but necessary. Home Rule was inconceivable after 1886 without Liberal support, and when the Roman Catholic bishops also declared Parnell's unfitness to lead the party, the great majority left him. With only twenty-six members of the parliamentary party remaining loyal, Parnell married Mrs. O'Shea and worked on. But the strain and overwork affected his health, and he died in the autumn of 1891.

Parnell had made Home Rule a major issue in British politics. As Gladstone said, 'Parnell did for Home Rule something like what Cobden did for Free Trade—set the argument on its legs'. But though the battle was Parnell's, victory he never saw. Indeed victory as he envisaged it was never achieved, for without him it was to prove impossible. As O'Hegarty has concluded, 'With him died, in effect, Home Rule, though the ghost of the movement, a pallid and an anaemic ghost, continued to dominate the political scene for another twenty-five years.'

4 Gladstone and the opposition to Home Rule Given Gladstone's prestige, energy and confidence in the rightness of his policy, it is pertinent to ask why he never achieved Home Rule for Ireland. The tactical mistakes of both Parnell and Gladstone have already been examined, but they are only a partial explanation, for they ignore the opposition to Home Rule. The opposition of the Conservatives once Gladstone's conversion was announced was inevitable, but why was that opposition so implacable? Much can be learnt from studying Lord Randolph Churchill's views. Many of the Whig aristocracy, led by Hartington, could also be expected to oppose Home Rule. Yet despite this opposition it is usually Joseph Chamberlain who is given the credit for killing Home Rule.

When ninety-two Liberals voted with Chamberlain against the 1886 Home Rule Bill, he thwarted Gladstone's grand design to conciliate the Irish by timely concessions. O'Hegarty along with other Irish historians has no doubt that Chamberlain's opposition was the result of pure ambition. Dilke, generally accepted as Gladstone's successor, had fallen when involved in a divorce case, and this opened up the leadership to Chamberlain. O'Hegarty finds it 'impossible not to lean to the conclusion that the deciding factor in Chamberlain's career, the wrecking of Home Rule and the Liberal party, was the belief that the summit of his political ambition was now within his grasp, were he but bold enough'. Certainly Chamberlain was ambitious, and with Dilke no longer in the running he resented the compliments showered on Rosebery and was jealous of Morley's promotion. Perhaps his rigid insistence on the distinction between Home Rule and his own ideas of federal devolution was reinforced by his growing personal antagonism to Gladstone. Morley described him as 'the envious Casca', but Chamberlain's motives seem far more complex, and an examination of his views indicates that he had quite definite and reasonable objections to Home Rule, objections shared with many others, including the veteran John Bright.

Chamberlain entered national political life as an advanced radical. A Birmingham business man, he had first built up a local reputation as a reforming and progressive Lord Mayor of that city. He had attracted national attention as one of the organisers of the National Education League, and became a Member of Parliament in 1876. Chamberlain had then helped to create the National Liberal Federation out of the Education League, and it was through the Liberal party that he had laid his claim to ministerial appointment. He scandalised polite society with his republican views, whilst his belief that the state 'must intervene on behalf of the weak against the strong, in the interests of labour

against capital, of want and suffering against luxury and ease'
was totally alien to Gladstone's Liberalism, with its roots in
laissez-faire economics and Christian compassion. He showed
little interest in the Irish problem until 1880, when he accepted
office in Gladstone's second administration, and found that
Ireland blocked the way to Liberal reforms in England. At the
same time agrarian depression and discontent in Ireland made
their own claims on Chamberlain's attention, and he became an
advocate of pacification, supporting conciliatory and remedial
measures and opposing coercion. Yet even in 1881 Chamberlain
was able to write to Morley that 'national independence cannot
be given to Ireland'. Chamberlain's constructive approach to the
Irish problem lay along the lines of radical social reform.

Chamberlain was incapable of regarding the Irish as a distinct
people with the inherent rights of an independent community.
Instead of Home Rule, he proposed federal devolution, as part
of his 'unauthorised programme' of 1885, and including devolution for England, Scotland and Wales. Through Captain O'Shea,
Parnell was kept informed of Chamberlain's plans, which the
latter assured him would establish local governments 'more
complete, more popular, more thoroughly representative, and
more far-reaching than anything that has hitherto been proposed'.
Such a plan, however, left the sovereignty of the Westminster
Parliament unimpaired. Chamberlain was offering radical and
efficient administration, but the majority of the Irish valued a
sense of national identity far more than improvements in administrative efficiency. Parnell listened to Chamberlain, for his might
prove the best offer available, but he never wavered from his
claim that the Irish problem was a distinctive national issue
meriting special attention, whilst Chamberlain could only see
it as part of a general demand for better local or regional government within the United Kingdom.

Chamberlain's position was therefore clear and distinct from
the idea of Home Rule, for Home Rule meant separation, and
Chamberlain saw, as indeed did Parnell, that such separation would
be the beginning of a progressive, if gradual, enlargement of the
jurisdiction of the Irish parliament. This Chamberlain feared as

the overture to the disintegration not only of the United Kingdom but also of the British Empire. Chamberlain seized upon Gladstone's failure in the Home Rule Bill to include representatives from Ireland at Westminster not simply because it seemed constitutionally wrong to spend Irish taxes without Irish representation, but because this feature of the Bill contained the element of separation to which Chamberlain was most opposed.

Yet despite Chamberlain's definite views, and despite the fact that after Hartington refused to join the Cabinet he was probably the most important minister in the government, Gladstone did not consult him over the drafting of the Home Rule Bill. Gladstone saw him as an enemy on the watch, and was anxious not to reveal his plans, whilst he had already decided to reject Chamberlain's more modest scheme of devolution because, as Hammond has pointed out, 'Gladstone had seized the fundamental truth that an Irish programme must aim at satisfying not merely Ireland's practical needs but her imagination as well.' But in despising Chamberlain's insular arrogance and ignoring his plans, Gladstone not only lost the advice of a colleague who knew more about Ulster than anyone else in the Cabinet, but also drove him into impudent rebellion. It was Gladstone's inability to compromise, for Chamberlain was given no opportunity, which produced this fatal development. By going forward without consulting his colleagues, Gladstone had discharged them of all their obligations, and Chamberlain always regarded the Prime Minister as the principal agent responsible for the divisions of the Liberal party.

The rupture was a complete disaster for Gladstone's brand of Liberalism. Chamberlain did not expect Home Rule to divide the party for long, and warned Hartington not to give up his chances of the premiership when Gladstone retired. Chamberlain was baffled by Gladstone. He expected Gladstone to accept defeat and retire from the fray, but instead Gladstone identified what was left of the Liberal party more and more with Home Rule. As J. W. Derry has remarked, 'Just as Gladstone's advocacy of Home Rule had failed because he did not understand Chamberlain, so Chamberlain's dreams of a revivified Liberal party were dashed by his own inability to appreciate the intensity of Gladstone's devotion to Home Rule.' A man of passionate ideals himself, Chamberlain was never able to understand the appeal of other ideals for other men. Thus both Home Rule and the radical mission were destroyed by the breach.

Chamberlain, the new radical, was joined in opposition to Home Rule by Bright, the old radical. Bright declared in his last major speech: 'I will never surrender to a Parliamentary party from Ireland, one half of whom have the dollars in their pockets subscribed by the enemies of England in the United States.' The opposition of Bright, because less spectacular than Chamberlain's, is often ignored, but it was little less effective. Bright was an elder statesman whose prestige in the party was second only to that of Gladstone, and Bright's defection had a decisive effect on the 'trimmers' who were not sure which way to steer; Bright brought many of them to support Chamberlain.

Gladstone was better prepared for the secession of the Whigs, though the breach with Hartington and his followers was a more serious blow to the prestige than to the actual voting strength of the Liberal government. Even then many of the Whigs, including Kimberley, Spencer, Harcourt and the young Granville, remained loyal to Gladstone. The Whigs were split over the Irish issue, and it has been argued that with more time Gladstone could have converted many more to his views on Ireland. Hartington, however was the brother of the murdered Lord Frederick Cavendish, and it is difficult on these grounds alone to see him yielding to Home Rule. Hartington, like Chamberlain, would not surrender the unity of the Empire, especially after the violent tactics of the Irish. To him the Irish did not adhere to the principles of civilised government—respect for law, for the rights of property, for the rights of others to labour and enjoy the fruits of their industry. The Whigs denounced Home Rule as a step towards separation, as an attempt to avoid the payment of rent, and as the design of intolerant Roman Catholicism to seek domination. Like Salisbury, the Whigs considered the Irish as unfit to govern themselves as the Hottentots. 'So Whiggery', as Southgate has concluded in *The Passing of the Whigs*, 'bid defiance to Gladstone in the name of the Union, Landlord Right, Protestantism, Individual Liberty and the Rule of Law.' Many of the Whigs were alarmed already at the inability of Liberalism to resist Socialism and defend Imperialism, but the effect of Home Rule was to turn the gradual trickle of Whigs away from Liberalism into a flood by presenting a major and dramatic issue.

The split in the Liberal party in 1886 was a heavy price to pay for Gladstone's support of Home Rule. The party, with one brief interlude, was out of office for nineteen years. Gladstone has been criticised for his concentration on an issue which was doomed to failure, whereas if he had paid more attention to social problems at home he would have achieved more tangible results, and maintained the unity of the Liberal party. Like Peel before him Gladstone had smashed his party by a personal decision on party policy without reference to the constituencies. But unlike the issue of protection in the 1840s, which soon ceased to be an issue, the question of Home Rule for Ireland continued to be a real issue which encouraged the renegades from the Liberal party to form with the Conservatives the coalition Conservative and Unionist party. Home Rule was certainly the occasion for the Liberal split, but whether it alone was the cause can be questioned. Gladstone's pandering to the Irish was reminiscent of many of his weaknesses in dealing with the Boers and the Sudanese, and helped to confirm rather than to create the doubts some Liberals already felt about Gladstone's leadership. It could also be argued that those of Whig sympathies who deserted in 1886 were alarmed at the growing radicalism of the party, and it is doubtful if their loyalty to the party could have been maintained by abandoning Home Rule in favour of Chamberlain's 'unauthorised programme'. Furthermore, if Gladstone had attempted to rally the party behind a radical programme of reform, and thus take the wind out of Chamberlain's sail, it is possible to speculate that Chamberlain might well have sought another issue with which to challenge Gladstone's leadership. Perhaps better tactics in 1885-6 would have prevented the loss of some hundred Liberal M.P.s, but the party was already in a crisis before 1886, and the coalition of Gladstonian Liberals, Whigs and Radicals had always been an uneasy alliance. Perhaps

Mansergh's cautious conclusion seems the most reasonable: 'The influence of Irish policy upon the fortunes of the Liberal party may not be determined with absolute precision. That it was destructive is clear, but whether it was fatal is open to doubt .. Caesar's body bore the marks of many wounds; it is idle to speculate how many of them were fatal.'

The 'rebellion' of the followers of Chamberlain and Hartington defeated Home Rule in the House of Commons in 1886, but by far the most insidious and portentous intervention in the Irish crisis of 1886 was Lord Randolph Churchill's cry, 'Ulster will fight, and Ulster will be right.' What was the Ulster problem and how did Churchill figure in it?

Until 1885 Churchill had every sympathy with the Irish cause, and he was anxious that the Conservatives should settle the Irish problem by conciliatory policies such as improving education and municipal government. The Irish people, like the English, were to be appealed to with Tory democracy. Churchill was not in personal contact with Parnell before the 1885 election, but he helped to create the atmosphere that encouraged Parnell to opt for the Conservatives. Once the election failed to produce a Conservative majority Churchill changed his tactics, informing the Irish, 'I did my best for you, and now I will do my best against you.' With Gladstone firmly attached to Home Rule, Churchill realised there were more votes to be gained in taking up the cause of Protestant Ulster, and in February 1886 he wrote, 'I decided some time ago that if the G.O.M. went for Home Rule, the Orange Card would be the one to play. Please God it may turn out the ace of trumps and not the two.' On 22nd February he travelled to Ulster. Churchill only voiced sentiments that were already entertained, but his support intensified the mood of belligerence. As Mansergh has pointed out, 'It was this conscious endeavour to play off the North against the South, that did more than anything else to undermine the prestige and the good name of English parties amongst the Irish people.'

The Protestant minority in Ireland, centred in Ulster, played a dominant role in the Irish problem from 1886 not because it represented a fundamental issue, but because party leaders knew that religious prejudices were easily exploited. It should be remembered, however, that Churchill raised the Ulster question not simply to defeat Home Rule, but to defeat Gladstone 'before he plunges the knife into the heart of the British Empire'. Ulster was to be ready to fight, but not only for Ulster; it was to save the Empire that Ulster was to fight. Churchill and the English Unionists used Ulster as the occasion for opposition, but it was the cause of Empire which gave to Ulster and the Irish problem their critical significance in the history of British imperialism.

The Bill of 1886 gave little indication of any concern over Ulster. After all, thanks to Parnell's management, of the thirty-five seats contested in the province of Ulster the Irish Nationalists won eighteen. When the problem of Ulster was raised in debate Gladstone justified his neglect of the problem—'I cannot allow it to be said that a Protestant minority in Ulster, or elsewhere, is to rule the question at large for Ireland. I am aware of no constitutional doctrine tolerable on which such a conclusion could be adopted or justified.' Constitutionally Gladstone was right, but politically he was wrong. Some form of federalism could have been introduced, some concessions made, and fears for the future of Irish Protestants would perhaps have been substantially allayed.

The fate of Protestantism aroused the greatest enemy of Home Rule. Whatever the effect of the machinations of Chamberlain and Churchill, the desertion of the Whigs, the tactical mistakes of Parnell and Gladstone, the real and decisive enemy of Home Rule for Ireland was English public opinion. This was clearly demonstrated by the overwhelming victory of Conservatives and Unionists in the 1886 election. Lord Randolph Churchill appealed to the fears of most English people when he declared to his Paddington electors that 'Mr. Gladstone has reserved for his closing days a conspiracy against the honour of Britain and the welfare of Ireland more startlingly base and nefarious than any of those numerous designs and plots which, during the last quarter of a century, have occupied his imagination'. Gladstone remained hopeful during the election, probably misled by the popular support in 1868 for the Irish Church question, but he clearly underestimated the extent of Nonconformist and working-class distaste for the Irish. There had always been fear of the Irish immigrant workers crowding the industries and keeping wages low, but essentially Home Rule offended the arrogant national pride of the English, their pride in Protestantism and Empire. The Irish had demonstrated by their outrages and crimes that they were barbarians and needed the guidance of British rule. Parnell and his associates had bitterly and violently ridiculed English politicians, forgetting that the English people were behind them. To concede Home Rule to Parnell seemed like handing over Ireland to the king of the ogres.

In the 1886 election the Conservatives had a field day. Electors were warned that Home Rule would produce economic disaster in Ireland, and would lead to vast Irish immigration into England. The Conservatives claimed that the accompanying Land Purchase Bill would cost the Treasury £150 million in compensation, and even Irish voters in England could not see why the landed tyrants of Ireland should receive such a bounty. The Primrose League was launched, and the Primrose Dames, led by the Duchess of Marlborough, organised branches all over England, where the wives and daughters of dukes beguiled the humbler classes with tea and picnics—all to stop Gladstone, 'an old man in a hurry'. And when the election was over Salisbury became Prime Minister with a clear majority of 110 over the combined Home Rulers.

5 1893—a postcript   Gladstone did not abandon Home Rule. Despite the successful pacification of the Conservative government, despite the Parnell tragedy, he tried courageously to educate the electorate. Morley describes one of Gladstone's meetings in Birmingham in 1888: 'He spoke with great vigour and freedom: the fine passages probably heard all over: many other passages certainly not heard, but his gesture so strong and varied as to be almost as interesting as the words would have been. The speech lasted an hour and fifty minutes; and he was not at all exhausted when he sat down. The scene at the close was absolutely indescribable and incomparable, overwhelming like the sea.'

As the election of 1892 approached Gladstone was persuaded by his colleagues that there was no prospect of an overwhelming majority for Home Rule, and in 1891 he agreed to the Newcastle Programme. Besides Home Rule the Liberals promised land reforms, power for local bodies to forbid the sale of drink, triennial parliaments, universal manhood suffrage, elected parish councils, and church disestablishment in Wales and Scotland. Gladstone hoped for a clear majority of eighty, but though only forty-seven of the ninety-three Liberals who had previously voted against Home Rule were returned, the Liberal Unionists still confused the issues in the minds of the electors. The Newcastle Programme secured a Liberal majority of only four over Conservatives, but the eighty-one Irish members predominated over the forty-seven Liberal Unionists, and Gladstone became Prime Minister for the fourth time.

The main feature of Gladstone's term of office was his second Home Rule Bill, introduced in February 1893. The Bill passed its second reading in the Commons by forty-three votes, and its third reading by thirty-seven votes after eighty-two days of debate. The Bill followed in general the provisions of 1886, except that eighty Irish members were to remain at Westminster though they were to vote only on matters of Irish or imperial concern, and the two houses of the Dublin legislature were made separate. In addition the supremacy of the Westminster Parliament was resolutely affirmed in the preamble. The 1893 Bill, however, once again ignored the Ulster problem, for Gladstone was implacable in his opposition to the threatening tactics of the Protestant minority. After four days of discussion the Lords, with the largest majority ever recorded, 419 to 41, accepted the Duke of Devonshire's motion to reject the Bill.

Gladstone was anxious to dissolve Parliament and appeal to the nation, but his colleagues argued that public opinion was more relieved than indignant, and urged Gladstone to press on with the Newcastle Programme. The Liberals could hardly go on ignoring the claims of their other supporters in a policy which had produced division and no success. Although becoming increasingly deaf, and with cataracts in both eyes, Gladstone accepted his colleagues' advice. What finally led to Gladstone's resignation was the war scare of 1894, following rumours of a Franco-Russian alliance. Spencer, the First Lord of the Admiralty, insisted on laying down seven British battleships at a cost of over three million pounds. Gladstone protested, but his Cabinet again opposed him, and on 3rd March 1894 he resigned. He was eighty-five years old. His resignation thus followed on his failure to maintain the three dominant political policies of his life—his opposition to jingoistic fears, the cause of economy, and a fair deal for Ireland. His last speech in the House of Commons revealed the long political journey that the member of 1833 for the rotten borough of Newark had travelled. He challenged the House of Lords' opposition to Liberal legislation, warning them that they had produced 'a state of things, of which we are compelled to say that in our judgement it cannot continue'.

Gladstone's last public speech was made in 1896 in protest against the Armenian massacres. One sentence in that speech sums up his political insight and contains the essence of his undisputed moral strength—'The ground on which we stand is not British, nor European, but it is human.'

Chronological Table

1805	Disraeli born
1809	Gladstone born
1826-7	Disraeli publishes *Vivian Grey*
1832	Gladstone enters Parliament
1837	Disraeli enters Parliament
1841-6	Peel's 2nd administration
1842	Disraeli joins Young England Movement
1843	Gladstone becomes President of the Board of Trade
1845	Gladstone becomes Secretary for War and Colonies
1846	Corn Laws repealed
1846-52	Russell's 1st administration
1852	Feb.–Dec. Derby's 1st administration: Disraeli as Chancellor of the Exchequer
1852-5	Aberdeen's coalition administration: Gladstone as Chancellor of the Exchequer
1853-6	Crimean War
1855-8	Palmerston's 1st administration
1855	Gladstone resigns as Chancellor
1856	Second war with China
1858-9	Derby's 2nd administration: Disraeli as Chancellor of the Exchequer
1859	Disraeli's Parliamentary Reform Bill defeated
1859-65	Palmerston's 2nd administration: Gladstone as Chancellor of the Exchequer
1860	Cobden's Treaty with France
1865	Death of Palmerston: Russell's 2nd administration: Gladstone as Chancellor of the Exchequer
1866	Gladstone's Parliamentary Reform Bill defeated: Derby's 3rd administration: Disraeli as Chancellor of the Exchequer
1867	Parliamentary Reform Act: Fenian risings and outrages
1868	Feb.–Dec. Disraeli's 1st administration
1868-74	Gladstone's 1st administration

1869	Disestablishment and Disendowment of the Irish Church Act
1870	Gladstone's first Irish Land Act: Forster's Elementary Education Act: Home Rule Association founded in Dublin
1870–1	Franco-Prussian War
1871	Purchase of commissions in the army abolished: Trade Union Act: Criminal Law Amendment Act
1872	Ballot Act: Licensing Act
1873	Second Ashanti War: Supreme Court of Judicature Act
1874–80	Disraeli's 2nd administration
1874	Parnell enters Parliament
1875	Public Health Act: Artisans' Dwellings Act: Sale of Food and Drugs Act
1876	Additional Titles Act establishes Empress of India: Suez Canal shares purchased: Sandon's Education Act: Disraeli becomes Earl of Beaconsfield: Gladstone publishes *The Bulgarian Horrors and the Question of the East:* Joseph Chamberlain enters Parliament
1877–8	Russo-Turkish War
1878	Treaty of San Stefano: Treaty of Berlin
1878–9	Second Afghan War
1879	Zulu War: Irish Land League established
1880–5	Gladstone's 2nd administration
1881	Gladstone's second Irish Land Act: first Boer War: Death of Disraeli
1882	Phoenix Park Murders: Arabi Pasha's rebellion and occupation of Egypt: Married Women's Property Act: Settled Land Act
1883	Mahdi's rebellion
1884	Parliamentary Reform Act
1885	Redistribution Act: Death of Gordon: Penjdeh incident: Salisbury's 1st administration
1886	Feb.–Aug. Gladstone's 3rd administration: Gladstone's first Home Rule Bill
1886–92	Salisbury's 2nd administration

1886	Plan of Campaign in Ireland
1888	Establishment of County Councils
1891	Death of Parnell
1892–4	Gladstone's 4th administration
1893	Gladstone's second Home Rule Bill: Independent Labour Party founded
1894	Gladstone retires
1894–5	Rosebery's administration
1895–1902	Salisbury's 3rd administration
1898	Death of Gladstone

Reading List

There is a vast number of books involving Gladstone and Disraeli, but apart from the standard references, this bibliography attempts to provide only those books that will prove both stimulating and useful for further study. The best biographies are: Philip Magnus, *Gladstone* (John Murray, 1954) and Robert Blake, *Disraeli* (Eyre & Spottiswoode, 1966). The classic biographies contain a greatly more detailed account: John Morley, *Gladstone* (3 volumes Macmillan, 1903) and Monypenny and Buckle, *Disraeli* (6 volumes John Murray, 1910-20). The viewpoint of European historians can be obtained from André Maurois, *Disraeli* (Bodley Head, new ed. 1962) and Erich Eyck, *Gladstone* (Cass, 1966). Hammond and Foot, *Gladstone and Liberalism* (English Universities Press, 2nd ed. 1966) presents a useful survey, and N. H. Brasher, *Arguments in History* (Macmillan, 1968) contains two valuable chapters.

A general account of the period will be found in the two volumes of the Oxford History of England: E. L. Woodward, *The Age of Reform* (Clarendon Press, 2nd ed. 1962) and R. K. Ensor, *England 1870-1914* (Clarendon Press, 1936). Anthony Wood, *Nineteenth Century Britain* (Longmans, 1960) also offers a general account. G. M. Young, *Portrait of an Age* (Clarendon Press, 1936) still provides a stimulating and readable survey, though more recent research is embodied in two volumes by G. Kitson Clark, *The Making of Victorian England* (Methuen, 1962) and *The Expanding Society* (C.U.P., 1967).

W. E. Williams, *The Rise of Mr. Gladstone* (C.U.P., 1934) still provides a useful service, whilst John Vincent, *The Formation of the Liberal Party* (Constable, 1966) adds a new light. Maurice Cowling, *Disraeli, Gladstone and Revolution* (C.U.P., 1967) provides a very thorough account of the passing of the 1867 Reform Act based on recent research. Asa Briggs, *The Age of Improvement* (Longmans, 1959) is an excellent general introduction to the period before 1867.

The influence of the Whigs on Gladstone is discussed in David Southgate's *The Passing of the Whigs* (Macmillan, 1962);

E. J. Feuchtwanger, *Disraeli, Democracy and the Tory Party* (Clarendon Press, 1968) and Paul Smith, *Disraelian Conservatism* (Routledge & Kegan Paul, 1967) deal with recent research on Disraeli and his contribution to Conservatism. A. J. Hanham, *Elections and Party Management* (Longmans, 1959) and his Historical Association pamphlet 'Electoral Reform in the nineteenth century' (1968) contain much useful information, and indicate that continuing research in the field of elections has still much to add to our knowledge.

R. W. Seton-Watson, *Britain and Europe* (C.U.P., 1937) remains an excellent survey of British foreign policy, and his *Disraeli and Gladstone and the Eastern Question* (C.U.P., 1935) provides a more detailed account. M. S. Anderson, *The Eastern Question* (Macmillan, 1966) provides a more recent account, and R. T. Shannon, *Gladstone and the Bulgarian Agitation* (Nelson, 1964) questions Gladstone's motivation. A. J. P. Taylor, *The Struggle for Mastery in Europe* (Clarendon Press, 1954) examines the European background to the period, and W. D. McIntyre, *Colonies into Commonwealth* (Blandford Press, 1966) discusses the imperial backcloth. Robinson and Gallagher and Denny, *Africa and the Victorians* (Macmillan, 1961) enquires into the motives behind Victorian expansion abroad.

J. L. Hammond, *Gladstone and the Irish Nation* (Frank Cass, 1964) still remains a monumental achievement full of insight and understanding, though markedly sympathetic to Gladstone. P. S. O'Hegarty, *Ireland Under the Union* (Methuen, 1962) presents a thorough survey with much use of contemporary sources. Jules Abels, *The Tragedy of Parnell* (Bodley Head, 1966) presents the most recent biography of Parnell, and Conor Cruise O'Brien, *Parnell and his Party* (Clarendon Press, 1957) provides some detailed insights. J. L. Garvin's biography of Chamberlain is rather heavy going, but there is an excellent pen portrait in J. W. Derry, *The Radical Tradition* (Macmillan, 1967). R. Rhodes James, *Lord Randolph Churchill* (Weidenfeld & Nicholson, 1959) can also be recommended. Mansergh, *The Irish Question* (George Allen and Unwin, 1965) is a stimulating analysis of the whole Irish problem.

Index